THE
OTHER YOU

A Map Into The Universe Within

An Introduction to
The Linda Bullock Technique™

TESTIMONIALS

"One evening, during a stay in Folkstone in England, I had the good fortune to be at a presentation by Linda Bullock of her technique of the mind map of the subconscious. During the presentation, Linda demonstrated the power of the map, getting those present to experience its spiritual aspect for themselves.

"For me personally, the experience was so intense that I decided to ask for a private session with Linda. Two days later, guided by Linda, I travelled to different places in the map. At one point, we came across something that was not supposed to be there. Linda asked me to look for the source of the anomaly, and I found it buried deep, deep under the ground. Next, Linda asked me to look for the reason why it was there or to whom it belonged. Right away I had the answer. My subconscious sent me an image which explained the situation so clearly!

"I had been working for some time on a personal issue, which I thought I had resolved using a variety of different technique, including reiki and kinesiology. However, the map revealed that it was in fact still lingering, hidden, deep down. Guided by Linda I removed all traces of what was there and cleaned and put things back to how they should have been.

"When I took a fresh look at the repaired space, I experienced a physical shock which I felt in my entire body. I felt a strength like I had when I was a teenager. The dreams of success and happiness which had been washed away by life's experiences were restored. The map had given me back my power.

"Linda's technique empowered me, giving me the possibility to fix my problems myself. I was once again my true self, full of life and powerful! At the end of the session I decided to register as Linda Bullock's student. I am now a passionate practitioner and aim to spread the word about her technique as far as possible. "Even now, years later, I still feel that strength inside. Thank you, Linda, for this precious technique that has the power to change the life of so many."

Patricia (France)

"Back in the late 90s I was diagnosed with arthritic knee. Over many years I controlled the pain with exercising and painkillers during flare ups. Maybe three years ago (it is now 2021) Linda was invited to Kent University to demonstrate the LBT.

"At this time, I was in agonising pain and had been for some time. My life was now being affected in many ways, driving, walking, sittings, standing and even sleeping. Painkillers no longer had an effect. The doctor sent me for an X-ray which showed my knee cap disintegrating with small floaters breaking away. I would need a knee replacement.

"Linda asked me to be her recipient which I gratefully accepted. During the session there was a clear moment when a shift happened, for me it was like a flash of energy. I did not realise what had truly happened until I went to stand up. NO PAIN, and from that time I have not needed a doctor, an operation or painkillers for my knees. But my life as I look back has also changed on many subtle levels that you are not even aware of until you look back."

With gratitude and love - **Gail (England)**

"Not long after our last session together I had an iron check up. What was found was an amazing increase in my iron. I had two injections of iron in December but in the past, those injections were increasing about 10 units of iron only. I do believe my session with your technique I had an amazing effect. I have been changing many things, also regarding my home and my space. I have now huge amounts of energy. I am even writing you this email at about 22.00.

"All this to say that a friend of many years made me think the positive change is related to the Linda Bullock Technique™. She said "Laura, think, there was a change in your energies". I said "for sure, very sudden between February and March". She told me that obviously something was draining me before. I thought about the work we did with the lake area. It was so hard for me. I think this was it. We put balance there as well as my home, the garden...

"Well I keep thinking about you and all the future possibilities to access your training. Really excited!"

Sending hugs – **Laura (Switzerland)**

"After a prolonged period of depression and PTSD symptoms, I was recommended to Linda's work.

"After one session I felt somewhat relieved. After the second one I definitely started to feel significant change. After my third session I felt reconnected to my core self

"Having spent some time in and out of talking therapy and finding no relief, this came as a marvellous surprise, that one does not need to talk through old issues to get to the pithy parts of mental distress. The keys are beyond the narrative that has been running.

"In the golden room of the subconscious is the answer. It is simple and effective."

Eva (England)

"Who knows where life will lead you.. But I'm so grateful for it leading me to this amazing lady.

"The technique totally transformed my life... For me I felt instant results in all areas of my mind, body and soul. It's incredible, when working with the map and symbolism of the subconscious, how you can dramatically change. Each area of the map deals with specific areas of your world... peeling away pre-programming and past traumas with grace, ease and dignity.

"Thank you so much Linda for empowering me and never giving up... You are an incredible Lady."

From Karen (England)

ACKNOWLEDGEMENTS

Minister Lillian Hurst, MSNU who through her brilliant mediumship gave me the beginning areas of the mind map which took me on a journey to discover the universe within.

Graham Bonehill, MBACP a Counsellor who realised the benefits of the LBT when he said, "You have to get this into the world because it will help so many people and even save lives" and his wife Linda for her support and encouragement in those early days.

Sheila French, DSNUT DS, Hon adv Dip Platform of Ershamstar School of Mediumship in Folkestone, Kent, England, who invited me to share the LBT with her students, which in turn opened many doors for me in the UK, Switzerland, Germany, Austria and France.

Robin Emdon and Abraham Emdon MA for helping me get this book published.

My grateful thanks to those who gave me their love, support and encouragement throughout my journey sharing The Linda Bullock Technique™.

To those people who went on to become LBT Practitioners, using the tools of the Mind Map to help people in their Coaching and Psychology practices.

And to the students and clients who embraced the understanding of the universe within .

To Humanity

CONTENTS

INTRODUCTION

My journey to discover the other me began over 40 years ago, when I first learned how to meditate in an imagining, visualising way. It wasn't until some years later that I discovered I could also use this technique to reprogram my life and help others to do the same. Since then I have worked on it with countless clients, from all over the world, and refined the technique to the point that I can now share it with you in these pages.

The technique I discovered is a simple way to connect with your sub-conscious, "the other you", which stores all of your life experiences past and present and many time cycles, using its own language of symbolism. It is a process which can only prove itself to you by you experiencing it.

Your sub-conscious is a living intelligence and when you understand this subliminal part of you, the discovery opens up a portal to reconnect with all that you are, have been and will be. The Linda Bullock Technique™ is a mind map into your cellular memory frequency patterns, time cycles and beyond.

You will have heard it said, so many times, "All the answers are within". Well this map is a way for you to access all you want to know. You can discover not only who you are and this other you, but you can also explore the whole universe and discover the purpose of life and so much more. This discovery is not just restricted to this dimension of life, but all dimensions can be accessed by journeying using this inner visual map. Because you have a map, you cannot get lost.

This book explains the mind map and how to understand it as you navigate your way through it. It takes the form of a visual mind journey and explains how to access all the stored life information and teaches you how to understand the language of the subconscious and communicate with it.

It is an analysis tool but once you know your way to navigate the map and the many time lines, it can also be used as a transformation tool, to reprogram your life.

A lot of your past experiences, many which might be unhappy experiences, some caused by damaged people, become your life programming, creating your reality and preventing you from becoming your full potential in life. These restrictions can be completely and easily removed, helping you to regain your true, free self.

During my first journey I found myself in a garden and then walking past a wood to a lake, and then coming back to where I started. But each time I took the same journey, the imaginary pictures in my mind began to change, and I questioned why that should be. Why were the pictures not the same each time?

Eventually I realised that I was in a symbolic world and so began my understanding of this amazing inner world, what each of the areas represented, why those changes to the pictures were happening and what they were telling me. We are surrounded by symbolism in our earthly world and likewise the inner aspect of us is made of the same structure and intelligence.

So, now, here is a book to introduce you to the mind map of your subconscious and your spiritual connections. With the Linda Bullock Technique™, you can transform your life from within.

Linda Bullock, *January 2022*

THE LINDA BULLOCK TECHNIQUE™ MIND MAP.

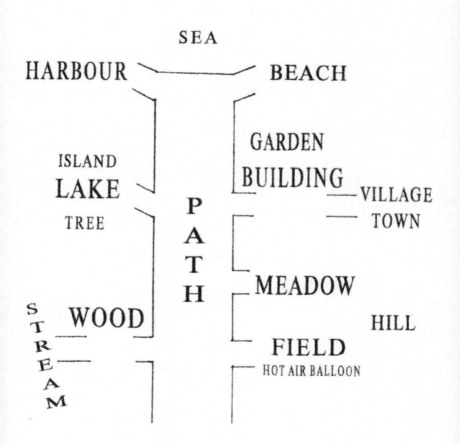

Chapter 1

ACCESSING YOUR SUBCONSCIOUS: WHAT YOU NEED TO KNOW BEFORE YOU BEGIN

The Linda Bullock Technique™ is a mind map into your subconscious. To discover and build the relationship with that part of you, you must learn your way around the map. Just like you are discovering a new place, area or town which you wish to become familiar with, so you cannot get lost. By learning this map by heart, you will discover not only the areas relevant to the present time in your life but also the amazing store of the past, and other time, connections of your life experiences and how you can access them through this mind travel. Within you is a whole universe of knowledge about yourself and your life and so much more.

At first, when you go onto any area of the map you are presented with the time frame which represents your "present time you", and your present experiences of life.

The complex communication with your subconscious might seem an enormous task to take on, like learning another language. It consists of pictures which are symbols which have to be interpreted using the character of those symbols.

In this book I cannot cover all examples of pictures you may see, but I have given details of how to interpret those pictures, so you can always check other symbols by researching on the internet or in books.

When you advance your understanding, you will discover that your subconscious intelligence helps you every step of the way as you learn to communicate with it.

It is not only the picture information you are presented with which can be understood, but also as you are in each area, you may encounter feelings relevant to that information like sadness, apprehension, tiredness, fear, confusion, feeling lost and despair, which all need to be taken into consideration as part of the information. Even a reluctance to enter the map or a particular area of the map is a feeling connected with that.

If you have these types of strong feelings while on the map, you might find it difficult to work close to the picture but if you elevate a little distance from the picture you should have a clearer view and not have to re experience the memory feelings connected to the pictures. There should be no need to relive experiences but instead you can view them in a detached way.

Elevating also helps if you cannot see the picture clearly. The message from your subconscious, when not seeing clearly on the map, is that you are having difficulty seeing situations clearly in life. Everything experienced is information and so any difficulties you might encounter are part of that information.

If you wish to see beneath any area, like under the stream or at the bottom of the harbour water, you can use X-ray vision and you may also ask for an expert. This expert will be a symbol also, for example a landscape expert or a financial advisor. Your subconscious is like Google and when you ask for an expert, your subconscious intelligence knows exactly what is required. This level of your consciousness is connected to all knowledge.

The Mind Map into our subconscious takes the form it does for many reasons. It is correct that we could take each area "off the map" and use those areas individually but it does not allow the interconnections of the areas to give a bigger picture and therefore it creates restrictions of information.

The wood, stream and lake areas are positioned to allow the picture to give us the added information of how something like sometimes the stream may overflow into the wood or travel to the lake, or even something, like the lake draining underground to the building or the village/town etc.

It has been suggested that the areas can be rearranged but I do not believe that could ever work. Its creation is unique and while it takes a simple form, we must also recognise that it is complex.

As we enter each area on the ground level, everything we see is relevant to that area. For instance, if we see a stream in the wood, it is relevant to the wood and may have come from a spring in the wood and not THE stream. If we elevated just above the trees and see a lake behind the trees, it is not THE lake but A lake, created maybe from rain water, and is relevant to the wood. We do not see THE stream or THE lake until we actually go to those areas or, if we elevate high above the map, it is possible to look down and see all of the individual areas below us. In other words we can see the whole map.

The wood, stream and lake are in the order they are because it is important that we first look at our wood and make changes to build our confidence by making sure that all the trees are strong and healthy and have enough room, light and all the nutrients they need, so they can grow to their full potential, before we go to the stream to look at our emotions. Only after we have made changes to these two areas, will we be ready to look at the Lake area which represents how balanced we are and of course can show depression. So there is perfect order to the map.

Being Guided on the Mind Map by an LBT Practitioner

The Linda Bullock Technique™ has trained Practitioners and you will find a list of them on the website which is *www.lindabullocktechnique.com*. It is often easier to be directed and helped to make changes where necessary by someone else. The LBT Practitioners have an in-depth understand of how to work on the map.

They will make sure you clearly understand the information you are seeing and help you to be empowered to make the changes to your life.

Important Information about How to Re-programme your Life

Be careful as any changes you make to the pictures on your map will impact your life.

It is important that changes to the map are done in a specific way which I have listed here. You do not have to make the changes yourself. In fact if you do, it is information that in your life you are used to having to do everything yourself. Your subconscious is an intelligence, an intelligent part of you, so you can instruct your subconscious to do as you instruct.

A law of the universe is "free will" and the conscious you is in charge of your life. Not even your subconscious can work outside of your control. So you make the decision to improve or remove part of the picture you are looking at and then instruct your subconscious to do the work. All of this is a mind/thought process and that is the communication tool between you and that other part of you. Your subconscious will use symbolic tools to complete your order. So don't be surprised if you see workmen and tools like diggers, skips etc.

Also instruct that whatever is being removed is taken completely off your mind map and therefore out of your subconscious. This includes not putting it in the sea or sky, although, I very often see anything removed taken to a light in the sky. It is my way of saying to God "please deal with that as I no longer accept it."

If you imagine a different picture to what you are looking at and put that picture on the picture you see, you will merely be burying the original and it will stay in your memory banks to still continue to affect you and your life.

Any obstacles or problems can be removed from the wood, stream and lake areas because those obstacles are relevant to "the affect on you", so removing something like rocks or mud or even a hole will stop them from affecting you. However also replace where necessary. For example removing mud might need then replacing with good fertile soil.

But be very careful when removing anything from the harbour, beach, building, garden and village without knowing exactly what the outcome would be. This technique really works! So removing say a ship from the harbour, and let's say that ship represents your job, that would create a situation where you would lose that job. A rule for these areas is "Improve rather than remove".

An example where you can make an improvement might be that you have a broken down building or ship and deciding to instruct your subconscious to repair and make good.

Do not be surprised with the symbols your subconscious uses to make the changes you instruct. These symbols could include workmen and machinery, suction apparatus, flying skips or any other symbol your subconscious deems necessary for the work to be done.

When working with the LBT with children, I point out that this is their magic kingdom and they are the rulers of it. I believe this is a good way for any adult to also understand the process. Do not be afraid to move any obstacles including mountains, volcanos, laver or even instruct the sea to remove itself from your map. Nothing is impossible when creating a perfect landscape.

You can redesign your subconscious and thus change your life. However, a full understanding of all the symbols you see is important and careful consideration needs to be made for the changes you wish. And never play with the pictures until you truly understand the implications of those changes.

How to understand and interpret the symbols

After each of the following chapters which cover each area of the map, I have listed symbols which you may have seen on your journey together with their interpretation. However, I have only given a short interpretation, and all symbols cannot be covered in this book. You can decide how much information you need for each symbol seen. Sometimes a short understanding will suffice but sometimes you may like to research more in depth information.

Some symbols will be understood by you in a different way than those listed. For example, a particular flower may have a happy or sad memory relating to a loved one, so this connection of the symbol can also be used as information.

You can check symbols in books, on the internet, on tarot cards like the understanding of the sun and moon, and anywhere you might be drawn for the information. Your subconscious is intelligent and because it knows past, present and future, it also knows where you will search for the understanding of a symbol

Numerology might also be relevant to be looked into. The energy of numbers can have a significant connection to the information.

Reference books about trees, flowers etc. will give you the character of each symbol. How it behaves, when it grows, how long it lives and what it prefers to be able to grow to its full potential and be successful.

For example:

Searching in a book about trees or the internet about a Maple tree character you can find the following information:

"There are many types of Maple Trees, the most common known as the Acer, although there is also the red Maple and silver Maple. These trees are considered a pioneering species.

These trees can be tapped to produce Maple Syrup from Mid February to late April and the benefits of Maple Syrup are many including supplying antioxidants, fighting inflammatory diseases, improving digestion and containing vitamins and minerals. However, it is better for the tree to mature before tapping it. So a young tree does not have all it needs to supply this.

This tree is most commonly known to grow in North America and was revered by the North American Indians and they used the syrup to barter with".

<u>Interpreting this information:</u>

All trees anywhere on the map represent aspects of you and this is made clear in the next chapter about your wood, so we would interpret the above to mean that you are part of a group or type of people who have the ability to help others to improve their wellbeing, including health. What you offer to others is sweet and enjoyable. "North America" would be interpreted as "new frontiers" and therefore you are setting out to change past understanding and discover and create something new.

Maple trees are connected to Celtic mythology and the Maple Tree was consecrated to Dana, the Celtic goddess of fertility, and this interpreted would mean that whatever this aspect of you represented by this tree, is in abundance.

Searching the internet for "Maple Tree Symbolism" says that this tree represents strength and endurance and is also known as the Tree of Tolerance and therefore you would interpret this information that these would be your attributes.

There is a universal understanding of symbols going back to the beginning of time. The Shamans of all cultures understood this language mainly because they were more connected to nature. They saw beyond the surface understanding of everything. So we can draw on and reconnect with this knowledge again.

Each culture understood their surroundings, so the North American Indians read the energy of trees, rivers, land and animals to see the connection which was between them. The teacher of the tribe would have a wolf's head/hat because they understood the character of the wolf teaching its young by watching its behaviour.

The Shamans of all cultures understood this mainly because they were more connected. They saw the courage of the butterfly as it faced death as a caterpillar in the cocoon, before it transformed itself, found its wings and flew over the world seeing it in a completely new way.

The Chinese horoscope likened people to animals and their character. So someone born in the year of the dog had a profound sense of duty and will never let those around them down. They are the first to speak out about injustice and are caring. Any animals seen on the mind map will represent the character symbol.

Analysis

To understand this language of the subconscious it helps if you put yourself into the symbol. Here are a few examples for you to see and feel the differences.

Imagine a path ahead of you. It is created out of large grey cobbles which are set side by side. You can see that there is no other way than to walk straight ahead if you wish to progress.

Now feel yourself walking on the cobbles. Experience what it feels like under your feet and the strength you need in your legs and ankles. You might fall if you do not focus by looking down and taking one step at a time. You cannot see what is to the sides of the path or ahead of you, only immediately in front of you. There is no colour on the path only grey which makes you feel depressed. You say to yourself "What is the point of trying to go forward in life. It is so difficult".

Now imagine a path of new green grass. It is a sunny, warm day and you can see the grass area opening out in front of you. Then feel you are there walking that path. It does not matter whether you walk in the middle or to either side so there is a sense of freedom of direction. The energy of the new green grass gives you optimism and a balanced wellbeing feeling. You almost want to walk bare foot to feel the energy of the earth to experience what life gives you. You feel the warmth and light from the sun and this makes you feel that there is an opportunity presented in your life which offers all you need.

Another example - Imagine you are looking at water which is muddy. Even feel that you are that water and see how it makes you feel. You cannot see what is in there and you cannot see the direction to go. But you feel the rocks which you have to bend around, which split you, and stop you feeling happy and content. You wonder which way should you go to move on from this perplexed feeling. This water pulls you down into the mud and drowns you and takes the light from you.

And then imagine crystal clear water giving the sense of clarity. You are able to drink the water and see through it clearly. Then become the water which gives a feeling that everything is as good as it can be. You can see where you are going, that there are no restrictions preventing the water flowing easily in a natural direction. You see the clear sky above you and feel the sense of wellbeing.

Another example is to see a tree strangled with ivy, with roots on the surface of the ground because there are rocks beneath it. There are many other trees close by which are creating a darkness because the light cannot penetrate. Now imagine you are that tree. The earth beneath your feet does not give you what you need and the rocks force your roots to grow out and above the ground in the hope that you can find good soil to survive. What goodness you have to offer is being leached by another plant which is smothering you. Your branches cannot reach out because there are other trees close to you and there is no room and so the tree feels restricted, confined and stressed. There is no hope for there to be the growth of leaves so no opportunity to succeed in any way. This tree cannot survive in its present circumstances.

Now imagine yourself as a tree, which stands in its own space with roots well planted in good fertile soil. Feel how grounded you are, with branches outstretched into the light and looking up to a clear blue sky, showing off new growth and knowing that it, you, have everything you need to grow to your full potential. You feel alive, strong, confident and happy.

If you cannot see the picture

Do not suppose that you cannot visualise. Everything on your mind map is information and if you cannot see the picture, your subconscious is still informing you of the situation. Step back or elevate and you will become aware of what is preventing you from seeing clearly.

Some Examples:
(a) Describing what you see as "Dark" meaning that you are "in the dark" to some situation. This could be caused by smoke or low lying clouds, or is it night time.
(b) Describing what you see as "Black" This would mean that you are not seeing any good in life and everything is negative.
(c) There may be mist which would be interpreted as emotion preventing you from seeing clearly.
(d) There may be an obstacle in the way such as a curtain or screen which may have been separating you from the situation.

You may like to travel with your mind to see the origin of the obstacle symbol you are looking at.

Instruct your subconscious to remove whatever it is completely off the map to enable a clear view.

Everything in its proper place

Everything on the map should be exactly where it is shown on the map and there should not be anything out of place or this is your subconscious letting you know that this needs to be looked at and understood. Here are some examples.

Wood – After you have turned off the central path into the wood area, all the trees and the awareness of them should be on your right hand side. If there is an awareness of trees on the left, these represent aspects of you in the wrong place. For example, maybe you notice three lilac trees on the left hand side of the path you are now on. Understanding what aspects of you they symbolise, which in this case is about sharing your beauty and fragrance but, in the wrong place, probably with the wrong people and a wrong person.

I would never suggest that a client looks on her left but instead, I ask if the wood is on their right when they enter this area. They will automatically tell me if they are on the left, or even in front of them. An awareness of anything on the left would need to be looked at, understood, and then realised that it is about being in the wrong place relevant to that.

If they are in front of you, as if you are walking into the wood, this can be interpreted as having to deal with aspects of themselves or, as this path eventually leads to the stream which is your emotions, having to not get in your own way to deal with those emotions. Again the understanding of what the trees represent from the type of trees they are needs to be taken into consideration.

Decisions have to be made as to what needs to be done to correct the picture so that all the trees, the wood, is on your right. Communication with your subconscious as to how to do that will be of assistance.

Stream – This should always be flowing from right to left. If it is from left to right then the whole picture needs to be understood. The flow of the water gives the understanding of time. So if the water is flowing from left to right, tracing the water first to the left of the picture will give the more recent past and then following where the water is going to on your right will give you where you are going, which is where you have already been. This represents going through the same emotional experiences again.

Correcting this picture required the whole story of the stream by travelling to find all the obstacles to your left and then also to the right. Just turning the water around in front of your will not be successful and might even create a bigger problem. This is a complicated area but here is an example

The journey of the stream/water from the left takes you to a mountain and a waterfall. This is the past experience of emotionally, when the water was running in the right direction from right to left, trying to climb a mountain, in other words achieve something, but as water cannot go up hill, it found its way into the mountain through crevices. Realise that the water was your emotions. Once inside the mountain, you were emotionally in the dark, in a negative situation, and could not see your way out of a situation. As the water/emotion filled the inside of the mountain, it somehow found its way out on the same side of the mountain as it had originally entered. The water was now a waterfall, so you will have had a big emotional drop, and then the water changed direction, going back on itself, and recounting how it got into that horrible situation of the mountain. You will be looking back emotionally realising that you cannot go in the same direction as before.

Once the mountain is understood, it can be removed, allowing the water to once again flow from right to left. However, rather than just fixing this one problem, I find that dealing with all problems the full length of the stream will help you to feel more emotionally stable. Otherwise all the memories of all the obstacles along the stream will continue to affect you.

Maybe the stream is coming to you from a giant waterfall in front of you, which would mean that probably there is an emotional situation which you cannot escape. It is necessary to know where that water is coming from but also check for water to your right and remembering to see if there is any underground, so buried emotion. Once the whole picture is understood the work to change it can begin.

Wisdom Tree and Lake – This should always be on the left, opposite the lake. Again, if it is not, there will be a reason why you are placing your wisdom in the wrong place in your material life. The path to the lake area should show you a picture where the wisdom tree is on your left and the lake is on your right.

The building – The building should be on the left hand side of the path to the building area. If it is on the right, it is showing you that wherever your home is, is in the wrong place. There will be a feeling about it that it is not right in your material world. Sometimes there might be a building on both sides of the path, one to the right of it and one to the left of it. This situation might be something like, you are still living in one house while a new house is being bought or built. Generally this picture is just giving the information as it is in your world.

Trees in the Field Area - This brings me to a memory of a client who I directed onto the map by saying "Step onto the path in front of you, walk forward until you come to a turning on your left, take that turning". I eventually discovered that she had taken a right turn. Just to be sure, I asked her if she understood her left from her right which she did. Therefore this picture was saying that she had handed over herself to spirit. She was actually looking at trees representing herself but in the field area.

A Lake where the Building should be - Someone who had learned all about the areas of the mind map once said to me that her lake was on the right hand side of the central path and not on the left. I told her that the lake area would not move, but instead the picture was pointing out to her that depression or an out of balance situation had destroyed her home.

A Stream in the Wood - It is important to realise that in order to move from the wood area to the stream area, it has to be noticed that you have gone "right past the wood". Otherwise the stream across the path and not at the end of the path is actually means you are actually still in the wood area. Check that there is still not a path ahead of you on the opposite side of the stream and be sure to have "past" the wood area.

Feelings and experiences during your journey on your map

When we are "too" close to the picture we are looking at, sometimes we experience feelings which are connected to that memory. These may be any of the following examples. This indicates that you are too near the memory, if so you can "step back" or "elevate" from the picture and the feeling will stop. Alternatively, come to the beginning, right off the map, and start again but this time, make sure you look at the area from a distance. Even create something like a cherry picker to climb into and be lifted to a position where you will not be affected.

Anger
Anxiousness
Apprehension
Cannot be bothered
Confusion
Depression
Being Destroyed
Directionless
Emotional
Fear
Giving up
Hurrying
Impatience
Lost
Nervous
Perplexed
Self destructive
Tiredness
Worried

You are pulled close to the picture

If you become aware of being pulled closer or into the picture, again it is information that you are or were so absorbed by the situation you are looking at that you cannot see anything outside of that situation. Step back or elevate to see the picture more clearly and therefore what is happening in your life.

You suddenly find yourself somewhere different from where you were on the map

This can be a replay of an experience you had which you could not cope with, and instead of staying present in the situation, you took your mind and thoughts somewhere else. In order to stop this from happening again, come back off the map and go back in but, this time, keep a distance from the memory which caused the detachment.

You find yourself dissecting every small part of the picture.

This is information that you may be acting out on the map how you normally approach things in your life, by examining every aspect of things in detail. However it may be that you had to notice all the details relevant to the one particular situation you are looking at on the map. If you find yourself doing this, you are not seeing the bigger picture. Step back or elevate and you will see the whole picture.

You are rushing at speed around the map

I suggest you are a very busy person if you find yourself rushing around the map. Remember everything you are not only seeing but also experiencing is information. Try to step back from the pictures or elevate and that should give you more time to see the picture properly without missing anything important.

You experience not being able to move on from the area you are in

Again, this is information about being stuck and not looking beyond what you can see but this experience on your mind map can also give you an opportunity to examine exactly what is there. Step back or elevate and this restriction will stop.

The Symbol of Words you might use to describe what you see.

Words you use to describe what you see on the map also have relevance and the understanding can be added to the symbolism. Here are a few examples but if your word is not on the list, look it up in the dictionary or internet to find other uses of the words.

Barren – This usually means being unable to carry or give birth to a baby, so can be interpreted as you not being able to create and supply new ideas.

Black – This could be interpreted as a black mood or deep melancholy and being unable to see any good in anything.

Bog – Bogged down with the heavy weight of life and your feet cannot find a solid footing.

Box – Being boxed in.

<u>Burnt</u> – Destroyed by fire and burnt out, meaning ruining your health by becoming completely exhausted through overwork.

<u>Cold</u> – This is being out in the cold, so no warmth from this situation.

<u>Concave</u> – Set Back.

<u>Dark</u> – In the dark and so does not see or know what is happening

<u>Dense</u> – This would mean that although you are not stupid, with this situation, you do not get it.

<u>Devastation</u> – Something created a severe and overwhelming shock or grief.

<u>Earth</u> – The planet you live on.

<u>Frozen</u> – Emotionally frozen out so being blocked so you cannot emotionally flow.

<u>Ground</u> – The foundation you stand on. Being grounded.

<u>Hole</u> – Seeing a hole would represent something missing.

<u>Hollow</u> – A feeling of emptiness as if life has been taken from you.

<u>Ice</u> – Ice is frozen water so it represents being emotionally isolated.

Plateau – This is a level of high ground not moving up or down meaning progress has hit a period of not moving.

Recess – A break between learning something.

Sank – Gone down and failed.

Static – Not moving.

Sunrise – This represents new beginnings.

Sunset – This represents the end of a period in your life.

Swamp – Overwhelmed and the water represents emotion, so overwhelmed emotionally.

Winter – A time of non growth.

The Sky Symbol

The Sky represents the outside world which is having an effect on you.

In each area, the sky is not all the same, so the following is relevant to the particular area of the map where you are. As you look up you may see any of the following examples.

Blue Sky – You have a clear view and understanding of outside influences or situation.

Chilly Atmosphere – Those around you will be creating a chilly atmosphere which you can feel.

<u>Cold Atmosphere</u> – People and situation around you give you no warmth of feeling and are cold towards you.

<u>Dark Clouds</u> – Outside influences are putting you in the dark so you cannot see clearly.

<u>Foggy</u> – This is usually low lying cloud and would indicate that other people or situations are creating

<u>Grey Clouds</u> – Grey is depression hanging over you created by outside people or situations.

<u>Hot Atmosphere</u> – You know the saying "things are hotting up"; well that is what others are causing you to feel.

<u>Moon</u> – This shows itself only as a reflection of the light of the sun and represents the dark side of nature and is therefore representing someone or some situation which is dark but pretending to be light or nice.

<u>Rain Clouds</u> – Emotions from people or situations outside of you will be affecting you emotionally as soon as the rain falls.

<u>Shifting weather patterns.</u> – There seems to be a lot of changes happening which makes you feel that you don't know what is coming next.

<u>Smoke</u> – This indicates a smoke screen created by someone or some situation, which causes you not to see clearly. You might like to look for the origin of the smoke usually coming from a fire somewhere on the map, which someone has lit. Fire means causing trouble.

<u>Sun</u> – Without the sun there would be no life, so this represents situations giving you what you need to live. It is a life giving force for you and your life.

<u>Stars</u> – These can be seen when it is dark, so when you are in the dark or when not much is happening in your life, it represents people or something good and positive given to you.

<u>Storm Clouds</u> – There are storms created by others, perhaps arguments and disagreements, which are building and affecting you and your life.
<u>Sun</u> – This represents light, power and warmth given to you and what you need to sustain your life.

<u>Warm Atmosphere</u> – You are receiving warm feelings from other people

<u>White Clouds</u> – These cast a shadow and make areas of the map beneath them less easy to see so represents a situation or situations which might cause you not to see certain areas of you or your life clearly.

<u>Wind</u> – The natural movement of air in the form of a current blowing from a particular direction. Also, it is what is needed in physical exertion, speech etc.

<u>Wispy Clouds</u> – Fine, thin or straggly clouds are outside situations which do not cause any or many problems to you.

The Sea Symbol

The sea is also the outside world relevant to whichever
area you are in.

<u>Choppy Sea</u> – This is created most commonly by the
friction between waves and wind. So the situation from the
outside world or others relevant to you, is creating waves.

<u>Calm Sea</u> – At the moment life around you is particularly
calm.

<u>Tsunami</u> – This giant wave is usually caused by an
earthquake under the sea. This means that there is a
situation outside of your control which could eventually
affect you in a major way by destroying everything in your
life. In this situation you can prevent damage by building
something to prevent it.

Underground Symbol

Awareness that there is a problem under the ground.
Request Xray vision to see what is there.

Whatever is hidden underground has been put there
because you wanted to bury the memory, probably because
it was too painful to remember.

If you become aware of a problem which seems to be
underground for example, a tree having difficulty getting
its roots into the ground, use x-ray vision and you may see
stones or rocks which need to be removed and replaced
with good fertile soil.

Perhaps there is a hidden cave which symbolises a safe place to hide and rather than just removing it, you will first need to check if there is anything in there because when you instruct your subconscious to remove the cave, it can only remove that instruction. Anything in there which may also need to be removed will need you to also instruct your subconscious to remove it.

You may find a person like a child or baby. Check by asking yourself who that represents and together with the intelligence of your subconscious, decide what is appropriate to do. It may be a lost part of you which was hidden away either by your choice or by someone or some situation which caused it.

Film and Story Symbolism

The symbolism of being aware of a film, a story or even fairy-tale characters gives a whole understanding to the situation you are looking at and it is your subconscious's way of giving you a lot more information about the situation. Here are a few examples.

Hansel and Gretel – After being lost in the woods intentionally by their father and step mother, these children discovered a house made of sweets and good things. Lost in the wood would represent that their upbringing was not character building but instead leaving them not really knowing who they are. The witch, who lived in the house, lured the children into her home by offering good things, but with the intention of eating them up meaning taken all that they are from them- However, in the end the children kill the witch and take her money and other wealth so benefitted from this unhappy experience.

Jack and the Beanstalk – Probably you have been taken for a fool by exchanging something of worth for something or no worth. However, by using what you have received, and using it to climb up out of your situation, there will be even greater advantages as you discover the hen (woman) who lays the golden eggs (birth of something new and precious which might bring wealth)

Sleeping Beauty – An example of this might be found in the wood and you may be aware of the thorns surrounding either a tree which would mean an aspect or aspects of you have gone through a wicked witch like person causing you to be prevented from seeing what is happening and disabling you or if around a castle, this would indicate the same scenario relevant to your home life.

Three Little Pigs – So in this story, three pigs built houses, one of straw, one of sticks and one of bricks. The wolf came and blew the first two houses down, destroying them and ate the pigs, so destroyed the people they represent. However he was unable to destroy the last one which was strongly built brick by brick. This is about building whatever you want to achieve strongly, step by step, brick by brick.

Yellow Brick Road – Think about the whole story and what happened. It represents the journey you are on which is a journey of the mind (yellow), brick (built step by step), and the journey is the destination because that person who you think has all the answers (Wizard of Oz) does not actually know. But along the way you gain a heart, a brain and courage. And where you want to get to is "home" which can represent a feeling that you have reached a realisation of "who you are".

Everything you see is a symbol

Here are a few examples.

<u>Bathroom</u> – The ability to bathe and be clean.

<u>Bed</u> – The ability to rest and sleep.

<u>Bench</u> – A meeting place to chat for a short time. Wherever you see one, it is often an invitation from your Subconscious to discuss a particular situation or event.

<u>Chair</u> – This gives the ability to sit down. If it is a comfortable chair it means you will be comfortable. If it is an uncomfortable chair you will be uncomfortable.

<u>Kitchen</u> – The ability to cook food and have everything you need to prepare and serve it.

Chapter 2

THE CENTRAL PATH

Before you take a look at your path, you need some basic understanding of the time frames and what the path represents.

This central path represents your path of life. As you stand at the start of the mind map, before you step on the path, the beginning of the path you are seeing represents the present time, what is happening right now. Further up ahead is your future. Behind you is the past but normally it is not necessary to look and be aware of that.

Always look at the path before standing on it. Otherwise you have already walked into the future. And also, it is not wise to step onto the path without knowing how it is. If there is darkness on your path, it strengthens the feeling of not being able to see.

If from the beginning of the path, you can see a long path up ahead, if means you know where you are going in life. If you only see the path immediately in front of you, it means that in life you are not sure what the future will be.

The path of life you have already walked is behind you, and if you turn to look, you will see that path. Your present day path could change day by day as your life situation changes, but sometimes it can stay the same.

If you cannot see a path at all, it has nothing to do with your ability to "visualise". It is information that you do not know where your life is going at the moment meaning no path forward. If this happens to you, take a step back or elevate and look again. Perhaps you can see more clearly what is there which you could not see before. It could be something like fog or mist or haze, or the dark of a tunnel or even a black hole.

Now help me prove to you that this works.

The Journey to the Path

1. Close your eyes but don't relax too much. Keep alert and imagine a path before you. Can you see it or is it easier to just imagine?

2. Note the type of path it is and what material it is made of.

3. What colour is it?

4. Would it be easy or difficult to walk on?

5.   And then open your eyes.

Now investigate and research the character of the symbols on your path. The internet comes in handy here, or reference books. You can even use a dictionary. Words we use to describe everything, can give more precise details.

Set out in the following chapters is an understanding of each of the areas and what each area represents together with short synopsis of the language of the subconscious symbols. If you were aware of the colour of the path, there is a list of colour symbolism in Chapter 15.

Path Symbolism

If your path symbol is not listed here, think about what it would be like if you walked on that path in life, how it feels, and how difficult it would be or how easy it would be. Is it a happy path or unhappy path?

Beach
Analysis – By the sea, either sand, pebble or other material
Interpretation – The best escape anyone can have. Life's a beach. Seeing a beach often represents holidays and enjoyable leisure time.

Black Hole
Analysis - Think about a black hole is space to understand this but also use the colour black which represents negative.
Interpretation - Therefore your path is informing you that everything you try to do at the moment just disappears into

nothing and there is a fear of you falling and disappearing into a negative life.

Bog
Analysis – Bog land was originally a lake area which has been built up with dead plant material.

Interpretation - Everything you have tried to achieve and which has not been accomplished (plants), and that you have put so much emotional effort (water) into, has now become an impossible situation where you can no longer continue and are sinking.

Boulders
Analysis – In nature, boulders are often giant moving rocks carried by a tsunami or an equivalent major earth movement or created by mechanical weathering. They are impossible to climb over and are too big to be moved.

Interpretation - On your path this is a major obstacle which has been placed there through a cataclysmic happening and it is a situation which has stopped you in your tracks and is preventing you from going forward. You cannot move this situation and probably will need to go off your present path of life to get around it and go forward.

Brick Path
Analysis – Used for building walls and houses. For a path it has to be set on a good foundation.

Interpretation - If the bricks are even creating an easy to walk path, it indicates that whatever you are trying to achieve and the foundation work you have done is going well. However, if the path is rough and haphazard, whatever you are trying to build is not coming together very well probably because it has been too rushed.

A Yellow Brick Road

Analysis – Your subconscious is using this as a symbol of the movie, the Wizard of Oz. In Buddhism this road represents the Golden Path to Enlightenment.

Interpretation - You have experienced a tornado in your life and now have set out on a journey where you believe you will have all the answers when you reach the destination. But also like the film, the journey is the destination and the experiences of that journey will give you knowledge, courage and a heart. It is about finding your spiritual home. If you are wearing the ruby slippers, you need to look to yourself for the mystical answers

Chippings

Analysis – Small pieces of stones, sometimes called planings, used as a surface cover for paths and roads. This material is readily available.

Interpretation - You have had to plan (planings) and use all your experiences (small stones) to deal with your present situation to create this way forward.

Cliff Edge

Analysis – This is a high area of rock and ground which falls very steeply down.

Interpretation - There is a situation where you may go from your present strong position, to being hurt or destroyed, so a big fall. Unless there is a way down, in which case, you can "climb down from a situation",

Cobbles

Analysis – A round stone put down hastily and clumsily for the surface of an old-fashioned bumpy road. *Interpretation* - Your life has been bumpy, slow and a difficult way forward, for a long time and you have had to watch your step carefully, in order not to get hurt. You have had to make the most of a situation which has been to together. Always look at the path before standing on it. Otherwise you have already stepped into the future. And also, it is not wise to step onto the path without knowing how it is. If there is darkness on your path, it strengthens the feeling of not being able to see.

Concrete
Analysis – This is a man made material made of course sand, cement and water which is usually grey in colour. Concrete jungle - represents no sign of nature and anything growing.
Interpretation - At the moment your life is about a material existence and a bit depressing (colour grey). This situation was created with time, effort and emotion (the material mixed) in order for you to have a solid based material life. There is no opportunity for a new creative life at the moment.

Crazy paving
Analysis – This is created with paving stones which are broken into irregular size and shape and laid in a haphazard manner.
Interpretation - At the moment you are trying to deal with a crazy broken situation. You are managing to fit the pieces together and make some sense of it and even use the situation, in order to go on.

Earth
Analysis – The world on which we live our mortal life. Earth also described the loose substance in which plants grow. In electricity to "earth" is to ground.

Interpretation - You are close to natural things and are in at the beginning of achieving something for the benefit of the world. If the earth is fertile and moist, you have prepared the ground work for this and have all that is needed to progress. If it is dry the world has not yet supplied all you need.

Fence
Analysis – A structure usually made of wood or wire which encloses an area of ground to prevent or control access or escape. Also to fence can mean to buy or sell stolen goods.
Interpretation - A wooden fence means you have been instrumental in creating this restriction and a wire fence means that it has been created by someone else. If the fence is to the right and left of the path, it means that you are fenced in and you can only go forward on your present path of life. If the fence is across the path in front of you, you are being prevented from going forward on your present path of life. The height of the fence and whether you can see what is beyond it can also be taken into consideration. If it is high, you cannot know of any other option in your life but if it is low enough to see over it, you can see other options and it is your choice whether to take those options or not.

Field
Analysis – This is an area of land set aside for planting crops or is a pasture for animals. It can also be used to refer to a space within which objects are visible from a particular viewpoint.
Interpretation - This represents a part of your life which you have set apart which is designated for a particular purpose and that purpose is to create something of benefit. While it is contained in its field of understanding, there is no set

direction. It also represents something you wish to study usually on a natural or even spiritual level.

Glass
Analysis – A sheet of glass is a transparent material which forms a barrier which can be seen through and is often used for windows. Toughened glass is strong enough to walk on but anything thinner is too fragile to take the weight of anyone and will be easily broken or shattered.
Interpretation - If it is a sheet of glass, it means you can see beneath the surface of a situation in your life. However if you are walking on broken glass, you are hurting. Perhaps your heart has been broken.

Grass
Analysis –A low plant with thin green leaves used for ground cover.
Interpretation - This is a new way forward in life because there is no set path and you have the choice to take whichever way you wish. There is a saying that the grass is greener on the other side which represents things being good, and things are so much better now that there are no restrictions.

Gravel
Analysis – Gravel is a loose aggregate of small water-worn or pounded stones which are roughly put down as a ground cover and the noise when anyone walks on it mean everyone can hear them coming. The word can also mean to make someone angry or annoyed.
Interpretation - There is a sense within you that you have been knocked for six and you are being forced to make the best of a bad situation in your life but you are letting

everyone know that you are not happy and are even annoyed.

Grit
Analysis –This is loose particles of stone mixed with sand which is used on slippery roads to melt the ice and snow. The word grit can also mean having courage.
Interpretation - At the moment, you must need a determined resolve and strength of character to deal with a difficult, emotionally cold and unpleasant situation

Hedge
Analysis – A boundary formed by bushes or shrubs used to enclose an area. Hedge can also mean to hedge your bets.
Interpretation - This type of hedge has been cultivated to grow as a insurmountable protection and keeps everyone out. It may be to protect yourself against potential financial loss or other adverse circumstances.

Hill
Analysis – This is usually a rounded natural elevation of land.
Interpretation - If the hill is on the path ahead of you, you will have to make some effort and climb, without knowing where that effort will take you, because at the moment you cannot see what is beyond the hill. Once you have reached a point in the future when you have completed that climb (top of the hill) you will be able to view the results of your effort and know where it has taken you.

Ice
Analysis –Solid frozen water usually formed from rain water/snow.

Interpretation - There seems to be a complete absence of friendliness and warmth in your life. You are walking a slippery path and could easily fall and be hurt. There is a feeling of being left out in the cold and isolated.

Meadow
Analysis – An open, often flat area of grass and sometimes wild flowers, which is open to public access.
Interpretation – This gives a feeling of freedom and a connection with nature and a spiritual dimension and the God consciousness.

Mirror
Analysis –A surface which reflects a clear image.
Interpretation - This is a time of reflection about you, and perhaps understanding who you are. It could be about your appearance.

Moss
Analysis –This is a green plant which lacks roots, and in most cases cannot grow where healthy plants are already growing. It prefers acid soil conditions and where the soil remains moist. It retains water and absorbs air pollutants so can be used to fight against air pollution indoors.
Interpretation - There is a sense that you are recovering from a long period where you have been emotionally trying to make the best of loss of some kind. Your world has been polluted. When the moss has grown on stones (hurts), it would mean that you have been trying to cope and cover or hide those hurts. On tree roots and trees, you are protecting yourself from the emotion you feel. It is like saying "I am fine" when you are not.

Motorway

Analysis – Is a highway with controlled access, with several lanes to allow overtaking and provides for high speed travel. It has a hard shoulder which can only be used for emergencies.

Interpretation - In your material world everything you do has to be done at speed. There is a sense that when others fall back you have to overtake and get ahead of them. You cannot escape this situation unless an opportunity comes along for you to change direction – in which case you would also see a slip road to exit.

Mud

Analysis –This is a mixture of earth and excessive water, created usually after heavy rain.

Interpretation - Either it has been raining which means that there has been a lot of emotion from others or outside situations in your life, or if the water is from underground, then emotion from within you has made it difficult for you to move forward. You are "walking through a muddy situation" which is slow a messy. Nothing can grow in mud so this situation prevents you from achieving anything at the moment.

Pebbles

Analysis –Pebbles are stones which have been made round by the action of water, usually the sea

Interpretation - So life has been difficult, but you have learned to deal with those hurts. The size of the pebbles shows how big the problems are that you have dealt with. In other words you have rounded off situations which would originally have been quite hurtful. But pebbles are often found on the beach and it may mean you have time on your hands.

Narrow Path

Analysis –A narrow path would usually be a walkway for pedestrians

Interpretation - You are limited in extent and the amount of scope you have to move forward in life. Perhaps you have to walk "the straight and narrow" of life where you have to be proper, honest and have moral behaviour.

Road

Analysis –Describes a single carriageway, which has been built for motor vehicles to use.

Interpretation - You are presently, somehow, being carried along the road of life, quite quickly, and your way forward is smooth.

Soil.

Analysis –This is a mixture of organic matter and minerals in which plants can grow.

Interpretation - If the soil is soft you are in the process of creating something new in your life. The ground work has been prepared, and maybe the seeds for new opportunities have been planted. If you see hard pressed soil, you have been walking the same path for a long time and it is emotionless and there is no opportunity to achieve anything new.

Stones

Analysis – Solid, hard impacted mineral which forms these. Throwing stones would be intended to hurt people.

Interpretation - If they are along your path, it would indicate difficult or hurtful things which have happened to you and still affect you. The larger the stones, the bigger the hurts you have to deal with. If they are on the surface, you have to be careful to avoid them as you go forward in life. If they are bedded into the ground, they are hurts which you have made sure do not trip you up but which are still painful memories to you. Tiny stones which are easy to walk on mean you are using your life experiences to take you forward. The size and shape of the stones relate to how painful and difficult your path forward is. Imagine actually walking on it and you will know exactly what it is representing and how difficult it is.

Swamp
Analysis – This is a permanently waterlogged area of ground
Interpretation - This means you are emotionally swamped by life and cannot get through. If it has become overgrown, you are overburdened and overwhelmed by excess work or thoughts which prevent you from finding your way.

Track
Analysis – It is a trail which someone or something has beaten by use rather than it being constructed and it becomes a way that people can follow. It can also mean keeping track of something or someone.
Interpretation -You have found your own way forward, regarding your life at the moment, and you are leaving a path for other people to follow. It could also mean that maybe you are trying to track something down.

Tree
Analysis – All trees on the mind map represent an aspect of you, so you will need to check the type and condition of the tree or trees and where they stand regarding the path. The interpretation of the type and condition of trees can be found in Chapter 3.

Interpretation -If a tree is on the path, you are in your own way preventing yourself from going forward. If a tree or trees are on the side of the path, these symbols and aspects of you and are relevant to the story of what your path is telling you.

Tunnel -

Analysis – A tunnel is usually a dark passageway, either underground or dug through surrounding earth, rock or other landscape. It allows passing through a potential barrier. It is enclosed except for entrance and exit at the beginning and end of the tunnel.

Interpretation - It is quite possible that there was a situation where you could not go on and now you are in the dark and you cannot see any way out of this unhappy situation. However, you are hoping to eventually find your way out of the situation just by keeping going (looking for the light at the end of the tunnel)

Awareness of what is on the sides of the path and the sky above.

You will only be aware of the sides of the path or anything above the path if it is a relevant piece of information and very often people only see the path itself at first.

If you noticed anything on the sides of the path, and only if you did, there is extra information for you. An example might be grass, in which case you can use it as an opportunity to escape your normal way forward in life. It is saying that you have a choice and can move off your path onto the grass but probably temporarily or now and again.

Anything which you do see on the left hand side of the path is about you, who you are and what you try to achieve. If it is on the right hand side of the path it is about your spiritual connections.

An example I have come across on the side of some ones path, is a trench on the left. This person was in physical danger from people and although she continued going forward in life, she had the option to jump into the trench if she was attacked at any time. So she would step off her life path and hide away safely.

There could be something like a cliff or drop at the side of the path which would indicate a situation which meant you could fall. Perhaps there is a fence or hedge next to your path restricting you or preventing you from falling over that edge.

Awareness of anything above the path such as the sky or the sun is giving you information about the effect of the outside world on your path of life. Above the picture of the map is the outside world and this would be relevant to any areas on the map.

If you are aware of the sun, it is telling you that life is giving you what you need to be happy. It is bringing sunshine into your life and giving you warmth and light which is positive energy. A clear blue sky would mean that you are not troubled by anything or anyone relevant to your path of life.

Grey clouds would indicate that there are situations in the world which cast a shadow on your path making it so you cannot see where you are going so clearly. Even white clouds cast shadows.

Storm clouds are telling you that there are arguments or problems with other people or other situations which are having an effect on you. Those storm clouds may be creating a grey depressing influence on you and if those storms actually break and it rains, you will be emotionally affected. How bad those storms are, represents how much you will be affected.

Night time would indicate that you are in a time of rest and are waiting for a new day to begin bringing perhaps new opportunities. Likewise sunrise or sunset would represent the beginning or end of a day = the beginning of something new or the end of what has been.

The Path Past and Future time

Up to now you have looked at your path "present time". If you wish to move in time and look to the future, you would step onto the path and then "with a clear question in your mind" walk forward.

The future of our life is always relevant to the present so might not be exactly the way things turn out.

To give you an example of a clear question, it should be said, in your mind, as asking the time and relevance, so something like "How will life be in three months time regarding my business?" This is specific to business and specific to time. Then walk forward and when you feel you want to stop, there will be the answer. Before you think about doing this, ask yourself if you sure you want to know the future, it may not be good.

If you have gone forward in time you would then look at the path and understand what it is telling you.

I have already explained that the path you have walked is behind you. As you know where you have been in life there would not usually be a need to look at that past path. However, an example of when you might look to the past could be something like realising a stream was running along your path and the direction it is running is from behind you. So in this case you might like to see exactly where the stream started in the past and then understand that it is still affecting you present time.

PATH CASE STUDIES

Case Study example (1)

Hopefully you are beginning to understand how this works. What you are imagining or seeing is exactly the way things are. To help you understand how much information you can obtain from a picture, here is an example of a door on the path.

Think about what you do when you come across a door in your life. You go through it from one space to another space, so it is an opportunity for change.

Look more closely and you will discover so much more. Here is an example.

Break down all the aspects of the door you are aware of and research each of those aspects/symbols.

The door is on the path, just up ahead. So the door, or opportunity, for you to go through in your life is not there for you right at this moment, because it is not at the beginning of the path (present time). It is up ahead, so in the future.

If you can see the door before you step onto the path, you must already know that in your life this opportunity of change is about to be presented to you. If you only discover the door once you have stepped onto the path, it is an opportunity you do not yet know about but will discover in the future.

The path before you reach the door is covered in primroses. Primroses mean an opportunity to make an entrance.

The door is made of wood and, as all wood comes from trees, and all trees on the map are aspects of you, it means you have put a lot of yourself into creating this opportunity.

The door has a number of metal studs on it. These have been forged and are decoration but may also strengthen the door. This would mean that a lot of thought and work has been put into creating this new opportunity. However, another way to look at these studs is to realise that they have been "painfully" nailed into the wood (you) to present a finished door.

The door seems to be an arched church entrance door. This means that the door on your path is relevant to your beliefs or your religion. Religion in the dictionary means the pursuit or interest followed with great devotion and the knowledge you have about it. Such doors are called royal doors or holy doors and beyond those doors is a place of assembly where people meet to share love and devotion for a greater understanding.

They are double doors meaning a combination of two aspects that have been created together. Will you be opening only one or both doors together?

The doors are solid and closed, so it is not possible to see through them to see what is on the other side. So exactly what will be through those doors is not yet known.

The doors are not locked but to open them they would need to be pulled open and not pushed open, so the new opportunity needs to be welcomed by you. When you opportunity comes, you would need be open to that opportunity and take it. If you needed to push them open, more effort may be required, or will the doors be opened for you so no effort needed from you? You will be able to just walk through them

Case Study example (2)

Looking at the path before stepping onto it, there is what is described as a black hole.

Astronomically a black hole is extremely dense and has a high gravitational field which nothing, not even light can escape. Whatever falls into it is trapped and cannot escape. So immediately, there is the experience of being lost in negativity (black) which would suggest not being able to escape no matter what you do.

Because a hole cannot be filled, it was necessary to remove all of the black hole, build a foundation (ground) and create a completely different way forward.

THE THREE INNER AREAS REPRESENTING YOU

Wood, Stream, Lake

Chapter 3

THE WOOD AREA

Every tree is an aspect of you and represents each experience of life which has made you who you are. The whole wood is the sum total of you. As you stand on the path in front of the wood to look at the trees, you are looking at those aspects of you which you are showing to the world and which you are predominantly using at the moment so your present moment self.

When you elevate above the canopy of the trees and see behind the trees at the front of the wood, you are looking at the past you, but these aspects are still very much relevant in your life at the moment. You will not see the whole of your past. Much of who you have been will be stored within the time frames out of sight.

Your wood might have one type of tree or many types, and what each represents, can be understood when you research them.

Seeing a path going into the wood is telling you that there is an opportunity right now to take a way forward and because it is in the wood, it is going to be a journey of experience to add to the aspects of who you are. Following the path will take you into the future.

Note - Trees found anywhere on the map represent aspects of you.

The Journey to the Wood

In order to get to your wood, you will need to step onto the main central path, but this time, do not look at the path but instead step onto "a path" and not "the path". You mind is navigating exactly where you are going, so the decision for a path will mean that your subconscious creates exactly what you are asking for.

1. Close your eyes and step onto "a" path in front of you. Walk forward until you come to a turning on your left. Take that left turn and walk a little way along it.

2. Are the trees or wood/forest on your right? Do not try to look on your left but you may naturally notice something there. Leave this for the moment if you do.

3. Turn and look at the wood on your right hand side.

4. Become aware of the whole picture and if you are interested to know what type of trees they are – just

ask and the answer will come straight into your mind.

5. After you have viewed that picture, elevate so you can see from above the canopy of the trees, staying just above the path. Look at the whole area of the wood and memorise the picture. From here you will only see the wood area and cannot see any of the other areas.

6. Come back onto the ground in front of the wood.

7. Only if you noticed something on the left hand side of the path, turn and look to see what is there. Also elevate to see what is behind that front picture.

8. Now, back on the ground, make your way back along the path and turn right onto the main central path and back to the beginning.

9. And then open your eyes.

When you turned onto the path on your left from the central path, the wood you saw should always be on the right hand side of that path. Everything in the mind map has its proper place and anything in the "wrong" place is information saying exactly that. So trees on the left or anything else you are aware of on the left, are in the wrong place. This means that whatever those aspects of you are, either you don't feel you are where you should be relevant to what they represent, or you may not have realised but the picture is informing you that you are not where they should be.

As you enter each of the areas on the map, you can only see everything in that area and the wood area ideally should be full of trees. Here are a few examples of what you may have seen. If you are in a good place in life, the perfect picture would be that all the trees are on the right hand side and each tree has enough space, light and nutrients to grow to its full potential. In other words, you would have reached your full potential and be living a very successful life.

A perfect wood would be one where all the trees have enough space and light and nutrients to be able to grow to their full potential. You should be able to walk into the wood, if you wanted to, in any direction easily. However don't try to go into the back part of wood by walking into it but instead always elevate to see it or travel over it. If there is something like a jungle or bog in there, it is not wise to find yourself there in the middle of either and your perspective is very limited meaning you do not know how big or small the area is from the ground view.

If as you enter the wood area you notice trees directly in front of you on the path, this would indicate that you have to deal with yourself getting in the way before you can look at your emotions which is the next area on the map.

Below are listed a synopsis of what trees represent.

Tree Symbolism

Acacia is a fire resistant tree meaning you are probably hard working but will not burn out by doing too much. Some species have sharp thorns and it is believed that Christ's crown was woven from it and if your tree or trees have thorns it would indicate that you are also capable of sacrificing yourself for the good of others. Its seeds can be used for food and therefore whatever you produce feeds people or gives them what they need. This could even be knowledge. The tree is telling you that you have endurance.

Apple is the tree of knowledge and love. This tree goes through stages of being barren, then blossoming and then bearing fruit and depending on the stage of the tree, that is telling you that you are either not sharing the knowledge you have or you are in the process of blossoming that knowledge or, once the fruit is there, you are sharing you knowledge. "An apple a day keeps the doctor away" which indicates that you that in some way you are good for peoples' health.

Ash is strong enough to stand alone and triumph over difficulties. You are tall and have ancient knowledge. When you are cut down you spring up as a young sapling and a new tree is born. A baby was passed through a split in the tree which was for healing and rebirth so using the baby as a symbol of something new which you create, you benefit others with healing of some kind.

Baobab is known as the upside down tree and the tree of life. You might look as if you are burying your head in the sand but your approach to everything is different from other people. In Africa villages are usually built wherever there is one of these trees. It blooms every fifty years and produces fruit which is considered to be a super food and is like magic for health. So people are drawn to be near you and are prepared to wait for the fruits of your labour which you can give them.

Beech is known as the goddess tree and is known for wisdom of the written word and study. It casts a shadow beneath it deterring wildlife which says you like to have your own space. Its leaves fall only when new leaves begin to sprout so you keep going with whatever you are doing before you make any changes which you will have prepared for in advance.

Birch is the Native American symbol of truth, new beginnings and cleansing of the past. You are tough, flexible and highly waterproof so can deal with a lot of emotion. The tree is also immune to lightning strikes meaning you can cope with other people's aggression because the tree is considered to be good to shelter under during a storm, you protect others.

Cedar tree is known as the timber of the gods and has been revered for its spiritual significance. The wood was used for the doors of sacred buildings and the tree was thought to be the entrance to higher realms. Therefore you epitomise these.

Chestnut trees produce a nut which is protected by a spiky outer shell so whatever you produce in life, you guard and protect. Children play with the chestnut and this would indicate that you might be connected with children and play. The horse chestnut fruit is poisonous but the sweet chestnut symbolises honesty and justice but you can be a little bit weak and vulnerable at times.

Conifers tower over the forest and they extends their roots deeply into the ground so you are well grounded. They are usually fast growing and therefore you are capable of achieving very quickly. They might be considered a tree or a bush which would mean you hide what you don't want others to see.

Cypress trees were worshipped by Diana, goddess of nature and symbolise a connection you have with nature. The wood can be used for ship building which would indicate that whatever you decide to do, you will never stand still but will create opportunities and always progress.

Elder trees can be called the Elder Queen and Good Mother who protects other trees and you must be respected and looked up to for your care to others. You create the energy to make the impossible happen and have a deep understanding. It has a multi stemmed trunk meaning you are a multifaceted person. The berries the tree produces contain antioxidants which are beneficial for health

Elm has rich foliage and sap and was sacred to Saturn, the Roman god of agriculture and therefore represents fertility. This means you are industrious, and capable of producing something for others. Because this tree does not rot when wet you are able to deal with life's emotions. Elm twigs can be used for divining rods indicating you have a certain intuitive knowing.

Fir trees are able to survive in challenging weather and substandard soil. It has endurance in cold situation and this is you. They hold their cones upright with pride and so you should because you have coped with so much and yet still succeeded.

Flamboyant also known as the Royal Poinciana and Flame of the Forest has a tangled trunk, roots and branches with a display of flame orange flowers in summer. Seeing this tree shows a difficult journey from the beginning and through time but if flowering, you have reached the ultimate presentation and can now show how amazing you are.

Larch trees are mountaineers looking down on people and situations and are often seen as protectors. Its leaf fall is wonderful for fertilising the soil so indicates that you give your time and energy to future production. Because the wood is waterproof and does not have knots, it is perfect for building yachts and other small boats. The lack of knots can mean you do not hold on to old hurts and experiences.

Magnolia is the Queen among the flowering trees and its flowers are called the crown jewels. When you show yourself to the world, you are larger than life and you have within you jewel-like seeds representing your achievements and these will be recognised as being precious.

Mahogany has a strength which cannot fail and is used to create some of the finest furniture. Whatever you give your time to, the results will be perfect and strong. These trees live far apart from each other and stand alone.

Maple is about being honoured for your generosity because whatever you produce is sweet-tasting for people. Its seeds are like keys so you are capable of unlocking many doors for you and others to go through. The wood is often used to make musical instruments and you music to peoples' ears.

<u>Oak</u> trees symbolise great importance and strength. They are hardy and anchored by a network of roots which means you have used the many experiences of life to build who you are. You have great wisdom and are the storehouse of knowledge having dealt with and endured life experiences.

<u>Palm</u> trees are known as the tree of paradise. It has a restricted root and copes with heat and lack of water. This means you can deal with the heat of life and survive when life does not give you much emotion. Even when laden with heavy fruit you still cope and in these circumstances you stand in your own awareness of good things.

<u>Pine</u> trees have healing capability as their scent decongests lungs, boosts immune system, balances hormones and is a cure for almost everything, so these must be capabilities you have. You need to be where you feel happy but if forced into being somewhere you would feel miserable.

<u>Poplar</u> trees do not look like they can withstand wind but its roots can spread far and wide and it has amazing strength because it can bend but not break. Its seeds are like fluffy white tufts which blow in the wind, so you are happy to let your seeds of knowledge go to wherever they happen to land. People tie a ribbon to this tree in memory of someone or something lost or for showing their respect.

<u>Sequoia</u> or <u>Giant Redwood</u> trees are the biggest trees in the world so you are a giant among men. Its roots never die even if the tree it dies or is chopped down so whatever you do in life, you will leave a legacy.

<u>Sycamore</u> grows tall with outstretched branches offering shade and protection. This is you and the connections you make in life. The tree likes to have its roots in water so you are happier with emotion in your life. In some countries it is known as the tree of life and symbolises spiritual awareness. You express old gifts in new ways.

<u>Walnut</u> is a strong bold structure of a tree. Because this tree has the ability to grow new shoots when any are cut it means you cannot be beaten. The nut shell looks like a scull and inside the nut looks like a brain and so symbolises an intelligent clarity and focus on life.

<u>Willow</u> trees can bend without snapping and so the message is that you can adjust with life and cannot be broken. You are creative and have an open mind to possibilities in your life and can withstand great challenges. It is said you can tell your secrets to the willow tree without it going any further.

<u>Weeping Willow</u> is so called because rain drops fall from its branches like tears. Perhaps you have sadness about life or someone and are hiding within yourself.

<u>Yew</u> trees were planted in graveyards and might represent the end, death and memory of something and a new beginning

About the trees

<u>Trunk</u>
Analysis – The central core and strength of a tree which holds the branches.

Interpretation – Determine whether the tree you saw had strength and interpret that as how strong you are relevant to whatever the tree represents

Bark
Analysis – This is the protective layer of the trees.

Interpretation – Trees with no bark are unprotected and therefore vulnerable. The question here is "what happened to the bark?" Had the tree been stripped and made vulnerable by someone or some situation, so it could be easily attacked and destroyed by someone with an axe or knife, or something like long lasting storms or lightening?

Roots
Analysis – That which attaches the tree to the ground to receive water and nourishment to the tree. It also is the source or origin of something. Tree roots are also the foundations of the tree.

Interpretation – This is about where you began and where you started your experiences. Be aware of whether the roots are in good soil under the ground which means the tree, so you, are receiving all you need, or if they sit above the ground, is it because there is some deficiency in the soil or even stones. When the foundations are not strong the tree and therefore you cannot be its full potential.

Branches
Analysis – These are part of a tree which grow out from the trunk or bow of the tree. The word branches can also mean part of any organisation and is often to as to branch out and make connections.

Interpretation – A particular awareness of tree "branches" symbolise connections you make in life. If any the branches have been cut off thereby showing a scar, that is telling you that that particular connection is no longer there.

Twigs
Analysis – These are shoot offshoots which grow from the branches. We can also say to twig something which means to catch on and understand something.
Interpretation – This would represent other connections you make and understandings you have.

Leaves
Analysis – Foliage on a tree. In the autumn these leaves change colour and are then discarded and in the winter, the tree is left bare and goes to sleep. The word can describe an extension as in extending a table. This can be used only when you need it.
Interpretation – When leaves fall, certain information is no longer there or needed. When in full leaf, there is a lot of activity and information, probably in the brain. No leaves would mean that whatever that tree represents in you is not active. If you were particularly aware of a new leaf turned over it is showing you have turned over a new leaf.

Tree or trees lying on the ground indicate an aspect of you which has been "cut down" by someone or perhaps lightning has struck it meaning something unexpected destroyed that part of you. You will know by looking at the tree how long it has been there and therefore how long it has been affecting you.

Dead trees – represent killed parts of you, meaning you can no longer continue with that aspect or aspects of you. I will give you an example of someone who had a dead tree. She had never learned to say "no" when asked to do anything but this had left her feeling "hollow" and "empty" and had nothing else to give. She had to recognise from this that she had to learn to say "no".

Telegraph poles which represent your communication capabilities mean you have had your arms and legs chopped off as far as communication is concerned. But relevant to that, that situation has left you feeling your life has been taken from you.

New trees mean you are still growing in that particular situation. Check what the trees are for a fuller picture.

Old Trees have been there for a long time and likewise you have been this person for a long time.

Strong or Weak Trees mean exactly that. You have a strength or weakness relevant to the type of tree symbolism.

Close together trees - If the trees are close together it would indicate that you have been experiencing a time of stress and if they are very close together, a feeling of struggling to get through and cope with life. Trees packed closely together are a barrier which prevents you from entering the wood in any direction so are telling you that there is no way through. Each tree represents you. The strength of the trees being close together means that they will not be felled by storms or lightning, for example, and will support each other.

Other Symbols in the wood and on the map.

Animals may appear in your picture and deepen your understanding of what they represent in your life. I have listed animal character and symbolism in chapter 16. An example might be birds which represent communication Now investigate and research the character of your wood and the tree symbols.

Artificial trees
Be sure to be aware if your pictures on your map are natural. Occasionally some people view them as "not real". Whatever things are made of are giving information. For example, plastic trees could indicate that you do not always show your real self and pretend to be someone else. Another example where someone looked at the wood and said it looked like a curtain with trees painted on it, like a stage set. Plastic
Material

Barren area
Analysis - Barren is a word used to describe being infertile and is often related to not being able to have a baby. Soil which is not good enough to produce any growth. Empty and of no value.
Interpretation –This would represent failure to achieve or produce something, particularly something new and would mean that there is nothing available in your life or support to achieve this.

Bench
Analysis – A seat made of wood or stone for two or more people. Also the office of a judge or magistrate.

Interpretation – This will be showing because of the need to communicate with another or others, depending on how many could sit on your bench. It would indicate that there is a situation where judgement has been made and needs to be resolved. If the bench is made of wood, which is made from trees, effort will need to be made to achieve this. When made of stone, it will be a difficult and hurtful encounter.

Boggy area
Analysis - An area of wet muddy ground that is too soft to support a heavy body and to be prevented from making progress in a task or activity"
Interpretation – Because this area would have been created by more water (emotion) than the ground can cope with, which is where you are trying to move forward, it represents you being bogged down by emotion and you are sinking.

Building
Analysis –The creation or development of something over a period of time which would be used as a dwelling.
Interpretation –A building or buildings represent your home and somewhere you lived and because it is in your wood, it is relevant to a situation which has impacted on you as a person.

Bushes
Analysis –Low lying shrubs.
Interpretation –These can represent an obstacle preventing you from moving forward and knowing what might be hidden. Something you have to get around. There will be a symbolic relevance if you are aware of what type of bushes they are.

Camp fire

Analysis – A camp is a place with temporary accommodation of huts, tents, or other structures, typically used by refugees, or travelling people. A fire is for warmth and protection.

Interpretation –This was or is a time when you had to live somewhere which was not permanent. If the fire is burning wood, the situation took a lot out of you to cope with the situation.

Cannot see anything

Cannot see anything – Step back or elevate and have another look. There may be something like mist or fog or a barrier preventing you from seeing. Here I have used Google dictionary for mist and fog and it gives the results here.

Mist

Analysis – Mist is created by hot and cold atmosphere meeting. It can also be a haze or film over the eyes, especially caused by tears, and resulting in something that blurs one's perception or memory"

Interpretation – This would mean that the emotion you feel has been created by situations or people "blowing hot and cold", causing a state of perplexity, confusion and bewilderment. Or there has been great sadness which prevents you from even looking at your life.

Fog

Analysis –A thick cloud of tiny droplets suspended in the atmosphere at or near the earths surface which obscures or restricts visibility.

Interpretation –In this example, the outside world has given you a situation which has left you feeling foggy and not able to see clearly what the situation is.

Haze

Analysis —fine dust, smoke, or light vapour causing lack of transparency of the air. It usually refers to visible air pollution, rather than just fog.

Interpretation —You are experiencing a vagueness in your mind or obscurity of perception; these are confused or vague thoughts or feelings. You can also talk about being in a *haze* when you're confused or disoriented.

A clearing

Analysis – An open space in a forest, often cleared for cultivation. To clear a space for something else

Interpretation – as all trees are aspects of you, those aspects have been cut down either by yourself or someone else and completely taken away. If this is a present picture at the front of the wood, there is still time to create something in its place. However somewhere else in the wood means that you have been destroyed at some time and this is still affecting you.

Dark wood

Analysis – A space with little or no light where nothing can be seen. Can also mean being deeply pessimistic.

Interpretation – In this picture, the trees and therefore you, are in the dark which means you cannot see anything clearly or at all. Has this been caused by the canopy of the trees being too close together and therefore not letting light from the sky into the wood? This would indicate that you have been thinking a lot or trying to sort something out but the situation will not have been resolved. I see the top of the trees as our brain and creativity, so if there is too much going on there, that is the information. I see the tops of the trees as growth of activity of the brain or mind.

Alternatively, is it <u>night time</u>? This would indicate that you are in a time of rest and are waiting for a new day = a new beginning.

Devastation
Analysis – The word means great destruction or damage or severe and overwhelming shock or grief.
Interpretation – Aspects of you have been destroyed or damaged by an experience which overwhelmed you and this has caused you to be devastated.

Field
Analysis – This is an area of land set aside for planting crops or is a pasture for animals. It can also be used to refer to a space within which objects are visible from a particular viewpoint.
Interpretation - This represents a part of your life which you have set apart which is designated for a particular purpose and that purpose is to create something of benefit. While it is contained in its field of understanding, there is no set direction.

Flowers
Analysis – These are something beautiful which have grown from seeds which were planted.
Interpretation –Being aware of flowers in general create a space of beauty and peace for you. However if you notice a particular type of flower like daisy or daffodil, check the chapter 17 because there is a universal knowledge of what each of them represents.

Garden

Analysis – a piece of ground adjoining a house, in which grass, flowers, and shrubs may be grown. An outdoor area close to nature.

Interpretation – Gardens always represent peace to me and if you find one in the wood, it is informing you of a time which was peaceful and when you could be closer to nature.

Ground covering

Analysis – the solid surface of the earth.

Interpretation – Awareness of ground covering is information about your foundations. However, all aspects of the ground covering need to be analysed. For example grass, bog, hilly, dry soil, water are all representing where you are standing in life.

Holes

Analysis – a hollow place in a solid body or surface a place or position that needs to be filled because someone or something is no longer there.

Interpretation – These can represent a feeling of emptiness and something being taken away, but also the worry of falling into a hole in life.

Jungle

Analysis – an area of land overgrown with dense forest and tangled vegetation, a situation or place of bewildering complexity or brutal competitiveness

Interpretation – there is too much going on in your life and you are lost and cannot find your way out of a situation. Is it representing a situation where it would be necessary to be ruthless and have self interest to succeed.

Lake
Analysis – a large area of water surrounded by land. It also represents your innermost feelings of calmness.

Interpretation – If you see a lake when you are in the wood area, this is not "the lake" as shown as an area on the map, but is "a lake". If there is a lake in your wood, you need to question how the water got there. Was it from rain or has it filled a low area in your wood from beneath it? There would have been trees there and have all been drowned. As water is always "emotion" in the map language, it would mean that that emotion came either from someone or something in the case of rain, or from your hidden or buried emotion which surfaced and destroyed you.

Meadow
Analysis – An open, often flat area of grass and sometimes wild flowers, which is open to public access.

Interpretation – This gives a feeling of freedom and a connection with nature and a spiritual dimension and the God consciousness.

Mountains
Analysis – a large natural elevation of the earth's surface rising abruptly from the surrounding level.

Interpretation – Some of the things that a mountain or range of mountains can symbolize are that they represent climbing over a mountain or passing through a range which is overcoming obstacles to make progress. Climbing up a mountain or other height often indicates spiritual or mental "rising" or improvement. – A time when you climbed to the top of your profession. When a mountain is in the wood but has no trees on it, it was a time when you had to put yourself aside for this achievement. If there is ice on the top of the mountain, the situation left you isolated and you felt out in the cold. If there are any trees on the mountain, it means that you also gained from that experience. Mountains can also represent someone with great authority or power over you.

An Opening
Analysis – a space or gap that allows passage or access - a beginning
Interpretation – This is a space where trees have not yet been planted and would indicate an opportunity not taken although there are possibilities or opportunities.

Path
Analysis – A way to walk along or travel on.
Interpretation – If you see a path at the beginning of the wood going into the wood, it means that there is an opportunity for you to take which is relevant to who you are. If you follow that path, you will be travelling into the future, even though you are going into the wood. It is all about mind navigation.

Pool
Analysis – A small naturally formed area of still water. To "pool" is to combine and group together.
Interpretation - Meaning a group of people working together and because of the water, it is with an emotional connection.

Prairie
Analysis – This describes enormous stretches of flat, grass or wheat covered land, with moderate temperatures, moderate rainfall and few trees in America. They are uncultivated with deep fertile soil.

Interpretation – This represents an opportunity to use available natural situations to grow and expand your ideas and capabilities.

The sea or Ocean
Analysis – is a large expanse of salt water which surrounds land.
Interpretation – This represents life outside of you – the outside world, because you are the land and it surrounds you.

Stones on the ground
Analysis – Solid, hard, impacted mineral which forms these. Throwing stones would be intended to hurt people.
Interpretation – they would indicate difficult or hurtful things, stones which have been thrown at you which have happened to you and still affect you. The larger the stones, the bigger the hurts you have to deal with.

Stream – This represents emotions affecting who you are, and discovering where the stream started will give you an idea of the story. If the stream is at the front of the wood, it is a very present situation. If further in the wood, it happened in the past but there is some connection with now. A stream which begins from a spring would indicate that some emotion sprang up from nowhere.

Swamp
Analysis- A low area of wet land where uncontrolled vegetation and trees grow and which periodically floods
Interpretation – Seeing this represents a situation where you are or were swamped. Because there is water here, it would represent an emotionally destructive situation. So you are overwhelmed with an excessive amount of emotion and

71

are probably "sinking". There seems to be no way out because the emotion from outside you keeps coming and coming.

Well

Analysis- A water well is created by digging a deep hole in the ground to access underground water needed to drink or for household use. Feeling well = in good health. Is it a wishing well?

Interpretation – A well in the wood area is about you digging deep to reach emotionally what you need for life. It can be about your emotional needs or even self healing. A wishing well represents a memory of something you wished for.

Wood/Forest Case Studies

Case Study example (1)

After turning left from the central path, the client, without prompting, notices that there are trees on the left and right of that path. The wood should always be on the right hand side. Everything on the map has its proper place and if there is anything in addition somewhere other than its proper place, it is information.

On further investigation, the trees on the right hand side look fairly strong, with space letting in light, separated sufficiently to allow each tree to grow to its full potential. However, what can be seen from here is an area of jungle behind those trees.

If a client is walking into the wood, they would walk into a jungle and at this point in time, it is not known how far that jungle stretches. It is for this reason that it is better to stay on the path in front of the wood and elevate above the canopy of the trees to see the full picture.

Behind what could be seen from the front picture, there is a jungle which covers a large area and in the distance, after the jungle, is the sea.

Then turning and coming back onto the ground, the attention is made to the left hand side of that path. The picture shows a few straggly trees which seem to have not become strong and the bark looks grey. There are no leaves on these trees. Again, elevating, there does not seem anything other than the original picture.

It is necessary to be aware of both sides of the path, so that there is an understanding of the pictures and then a decision can be reached as to what to do.

The trees on the left are maple and represent a situation where the client tried to share their understandings to help others but was unable to. The grey bark represents a depressing journey taken relevant to this, and the lack of leaves which happens in winter, means that the situation came to an end and there was no opportunity to continue. After dealing with the wood on the right, it was decided that if these trees were healed and found a space on the right it would represent a return to the same situation but with strength. However, the client decided against that decision and the subconscious was instructed to remove the trees and landscape the area.

Now attention was turned to the right hand side wood again. The client elevated and the following work took place:

First the sea was instructed to remove itself, like a tide going out, until it no longer existed. Salt left by the sea was removed and good fertile soil replaced it. Then the subconscious was instructed to replant the whole area with trees, giving them enough space and nutrients so they could grow to their full potential. The point of this was to replace the trees which were destroyed when the sea came onto the land. Early in the client's life, the world had destroyed the client.

Next the subconscious was instructed to remove the jungle and the water which was in the ground. Special attention was given to the storm clouds which lay above the picture and they were removed. Once this was done, again the subconscious was instructed to bring in good fertile soil and replant the whole area with trees giving them all they needed to grow to their full potential.

This work on the wood area was to put back the aspects of the client which had been destroyed in the past and was still affecting them. You cannot see the whole of your life experiences but only those experiences which are still affecting you.

Case Study example (2)

The client stops on the path and looks at the wood in front of them. The trees are set back and immediately in front of the client is an area which they describe as a cleared area. So that implies that there were once trees there which have obviously, not only been chopped down, but have been completely removed.

As the client is looking at themselves at the moment in present time, this is what has happened to them. They have not only been destroyed but everything which they were recently has gone.

The client was asked to elevate and look over the whole wood area beyond the trees in the distance and it was discovered that there were a number of areas where there were no trees and again, the client described those areas as clearings.

It is often the case that when something like this has happened once in a person's life, it is as if a pattern has been created which the client inadvertently repeats throughout their life.

To correct this programming, the subconscious was instructed to remove any of the people who were instrumental in inflicting this damage to them (removing those people from the picture as only removing their "effect" on the client), and then the instruction was to make sure in all the cleared areas that the soil was fertile and then new trees were planted, spaced to allow each of those trees to grow to their full potential.

This change replaces what has been destroyed, replacing the confidence in the client's capabilities.

Chapter 4

THE STREAM AREA

The stream water represents your emotions and the path of the stream represents the experiences and obstacles you have encountered emotionally throughout your life.

Be sure that you have gone past the wood area so the wood is no longer in your awareness or you might come to a stream crossing your path in the wood area. Each area is individual so make sure you have reached the very end of the path in order to have reached the stream area.

When you stand at the end of the path and look at the stream or river you are looking at your emotional state right now. If the water is calm, you are emotionally calm. If the water is fast flowing, you will be emotionally in turmoil and how much depends on how turbulent that water is. If you water is clear, you have a clear understanding of your emotions but if the water is not clear, there will be situations you cannot see clearly and which are affecting your emotions.

The water should run from right to left if you are emotionally looking forward to life but if it runs from left to right, you are heading for rerunning past emotional experiences. I have been asked if it makes any difference if you are right or left handed and the answer is no. The stream should be running from right to left.

If your stream is running from right to left, and if you trace your way along that stream from where it flows, you will see past emotional experiences still having an effect on you. If you look to the left from the end of the path, you can see how your emotions will be in the future.

However, if your stream is running from left to right you will have experienced some obstacle which stopped you from progressing and you will be on your way to re experience past problem again. You know that feeling that you have been through similar experiences in your past, well your subconscious will show you exactly what happened and what will happen in the future, unless you alter your subconscious programming.

The Journey of the Stream is the emotional journey you have been on either in present time, as shown by the stream at the end of the path, or in the past when following the stream journey from where it has come. If you are following the full length of the stream, you will not be seeing every emotional experience you have ever had. You will only be seeing those emotional memories which still have an effect on you now. Everything you are aware of is information and in the stream area any obstacles represent that information.

The Journey to the Stream

1. Close your eyes and again, step onto "a" path in front of you. Walk forward until you come to a turning on your left. Take that left turn and walk along and "past" the wood to the very end of the path.

2. Become aware of the whole picture in front of you. Look into the water to see if it is clear or not and how much water there is. Is there anything in the water?

3. Now look in the direction from where the water is flowing. This should be from right to left. If the water flows from left to right, after you have looked to the left, then also look to your right.

4. You can now elevate to have a perspective on the whole journey of the stream.

5. Now come back onto the ground and turn around and make your way back past the wood and turn right onto the main path and back to the beginning.

6. And then open your eyes.

Water Symbolism

What causes the water to behave the way it does and what is the origin of that cause, also needs to be looked at in the picture. It is possible to have x-ray vision if you need to look at the bottom or under the bottom of the water. If, as you look at the picture, you begin to feel any type of emotion, including not seeing clearly, step back or elevate. It is unnecessary to relive your negative experiences.

Babbling water – Emotionally thoughts are rapid and continuous in a foolish and incomprehensive way.

Black water – Emotionally you are in a negative state. Investigate what is causing the water to be black.

Bubbling water – Emotionally all thoughts of something expected don't last long. Bubbles are full of air so check where that air is coming from.

Clay – This is shifting sand particles for plant growth or to make pottery or bricks. Impermeable to water this must be an emotional experience where you have not yet created what you want to. In its present form, it is emotionally affecting you.

Clear Water – Emotionally it is a good feeling because you can see clearly and nothing is obscured.

Cold water represents a feeling of emotional coldness and knowing where it came from gives a bigger picture. Often it is flowing from a mountain where ice or snow is melting. As this ice or snow comes from the sky, which would represent outside emotional experiences which affected you and continue to make you feel you are emotionally in the cold. The water could also come from a melting glacier which is a sheet of ice which moves under its own weight.

Dark Water – Emotionally lost and in the dark.

Deep water – If you can see where the bottom is it means fear of drowning or having to put a lot of emotion into something to keep afloat. If you cannot see the bottom, potentially some danger is hidden from sight is affecting your emotions.

Fast moving – Emotion which is hyper and is running away and cannot be stopped

Fish in the water – Fish represent knowledge. If you can see the fish you will be putting your emotion into learning or understanding something. How that knowledge is affecting you is shown by the size and type of fish and how much disturbance they are having on the water, which is on your emotions.

Flooding water – On the verge of crying.

Glacier – Slowly moving mass of ice moving under its own weight. It cannot be held back and the conditions for a glacier are only found in high mountain areas. This represents when you climbed to a position in life and experienced an unfriendly and unemotional situation.

Green water caused by algae – The inability to put down roots in your life which causes a lack of knowing what to do.

Hot water means exactly that, you are in hot water emotionally. This is often caused by underground lave which represents buried anger.

Lake – When the stream has broken over the bed of the stream it shows a time when you became emotionally out of balance and depressed. If you think of a lake, it sits in a depression of the land.

Meandering water – Feeling no need to rush and taking life emotionally easy.

Misty water – If the mist is on the surface, you are close to tears because of emotional changes making it difficult to see clearly

Muddy Water – A feeling of emotions being stirred from deep within you, which is creating difficulty to see things clearly.

No water – Emotion has been either held back, shut down or buried so you are not showing any emotion.

Raging water – Feeling emotionally angry.

Rushing water – No time to spare affecting you emotionally.

Shallow Water – Not allowing emotional balance. Some emotions are being held back or buried out of sight.

Silt – This is clay carried by moving currents which can settle in still water and become siltstone which is a hard stone. Clay can be used for making pots so this can be interpreted as you trying to create something but which has been destroyed and has affected you emotionally. The silt might stop the water flowing creating a barrier or silt stone in your stream. This would feel like something solid has knocked you back.

Snow – Water which has crystallised in the sky and falls to earth. It delays growth of plants. This represents other people's cold emotions affecting you.

Stagnant water – Emotionally at a standstill and the situation is festering.

Still water – If clear, it is a time that you are at a standstill emotionally.

Swirling water – Emotions going round and round and not going forward.

The Stream Symbolism

Beck – This is a small stream so it is an inability to show much emotion. This can also mean being at some ones beck and call, so not allowed to have your own full expression.

Boulder – It is an obstacle from someone or some situation which stopped you in your tracks emotionally.

Bridge - is a way to get over an emotional problem by seeing the situation from the other side.

<u>Building</u> – Described as a "building or buildings" it would represent home and if the building stands in the stream and the stream runs through or into it, it represents all your emotions going into your home. If it is described as what it is e.g. watermill or factory or a village, it will probably represent work.

<u>Caves</u> - If underground, these would represent hiding places for you or someone or something. Check who or what is inside them using x-ray vision.

<u>Desert</u> – A time when there was no emotion in your life. Perhaps the stream runs underneath the desert which meant you had to hide your emotions.

<u>Flowers </u>– These have their own symbolic understanding which you can research of take a look at the list in Chapter 17 or there may be a memory which you hold about the flowers you see. An example - a flower which your mother loved and that would connect with her.

<u>Mountains</u> – on the path of the stream represent obstacles in your way or something you tried to achieve by climbing to a high position. Of course, water does not go uphill but often finds its way into the mountain and then out the other side. You need to recognise the relevance of the picture and follow what the water is doing for clarification. Mountains at the side of the stream might represent someone or something of power watching you or mountains which could have been climbed but were not. A mountain range can symbolise an obstacle in your way, preventing you from reaching the other side without a lot of effort.

People pouring buckets of water into the stream – This represents other people loading their emotions onto yours.

River – Unlike the bed of a stream which can only hold so much water, a river is able to cope with larger amounts. This means that you are able to cope with a lot of emotion without being overwhelmed by it.

Sea – The sea or ocean represents the outside world and life outside of you. If the fresh water of the stream runs into the sea, it is lost. You cannot find the fresh water in the salt sea water so you will be emotionally lost. If the stream runs from the sea, the stream will be salt water and this is damaging to the emotions and your own emotions will not exist. The outside world is in control of your emotions. Sea water is poison to the land and very often this person would not be well.

Stones – All stones found on the mind map represent hurts, as if people have thrown stones at you and in the stream, they have affected you emotionally. The size of the stones shows the size of the hurt.

Tree pieces or branches – When these are floating in the water, there was a time when you were destroyed and this is still affecting you emotionally

Trees – As all trees on the mind map are you, your confidence has had to deal with emotional situations you have encountered.

Underground water is when you have buried your emotions. Because you are able to see underground with x-ray vision anywhere on the technique map, you would know if that underground water was still a stream or had become a lake which would represent buried and therefore hidden emotional balance. Perhaps there are

Village – This represents a community relevant to your emotions. Becoming aware of the exact location of the water relevant to the village will explain how that situation has affected you.

Waterfalls represent you emotionally going over the edge and depending on how big a drop there is would indicate how emotional that was.

Waterwheel would be an emotional time of treading water to survive. In other words, working hard to supply basic needs. Waterwheels are used for milling flour which makes bread which represents the food we eat.

THE STREAM AREA CASE STUDIES

Case Study example (1)

The client stood at the end of the path and looked at the stream in front of them. The flow of the stream is from right to left but it is in full flood, about to overflow the banks. This is showing that the client is very emotional right now and could easily burst out crying. This is causing by a situation where someone who does not like them, has power over them and is on the brink of destroying them

Asked to trace along the stream to where all the water is coming from, the client sees that there is a tributary, which looks like another stream feeding directly into the main stream. The client is now looking into their past emotional experience but which is still affecting them now.

This was an experience where they had been in a similar situation where the emotion of someone else had been inflicted on her.

The water had been held back by a wooden gate = she had tried to prevent it from affecting her emotionally. But the wooden gate was now broken down and the water, or emotion, was all adding from that experience to her present experience which was making it more difficult for her to cope with the negative emotional situation.

It was decided by her to trace where the tributary started and when she found the spring which was the start of it; she instructed that it be stopped immediately. That created an immediate feeling of calm within her, ready to face any onslaught from that person in power.

Case Study example – the stream (2)

At the end of the path, the stream was seen to be flowing from left to right which is completely the wrong way that it should be flowing. The water was shallow although the bed of the stream could easily have taken much more water than was in it. So this represented the feeling for the client of being emotionally drained.

The client was asked to travel in the direction the water was travelling from. They noticed a mountain which prevented the water from continuing past it and at the bottom of a mountain was a lake. The mountain represented a situation where the client had encountered a situation of a person who had power over them and they were prevented from going forward. This was a very emotional experience which had hurt the client deeply. The lake had been built up and this was a memory from that experience and feeling that they could not go forward emotionally anymore and the lake represented them feeling out of balance with themselves and depressed.

The only course was for the water to come back on itself and travel back in the wrong direction. This represented the client retracing their steps backwards to find another way forward. Before removing the obstacle which was the mountain and the lake, it was necessary to check where the stream was now flowing to. To the client's right, which is going back further in time, there was another lake but beyond that lake running from right to left was a clear water stream.

This picture on the map showed that there had been another lake which was an emotional depression further back in time and that if the picture was not changed they would repeat old experiences again. Because the stream at the far side of the lake ran as it should, there seemed no need to travel further back in time than this. It is not always necessary to go back to the source of the stream.

The client returned to the end of the path and elevated to see the journey of the stream both to the left and right of themselves and then the subconscious was instructed to take out the excess water from each of the lakes and in the place of the land depression, re-level the land and create a perfect bed of the stream. At the same time the mountain was instructed by the client to be removed completely and again the land to be re-landscaped with a perfect bed of a stream. It was then easy for the stream to flow happily from right to left.

These changes were felt as a relief for the client as emotionally they no longer felt they were going in two directions with no solution in sight and being emotionally lost.

Chapter 5

THE LAKE AREAS

There are three areas within this area of the mind map. All areas are relevant to and represent balance within you. First we will deal with two of those areas, the Wisdom Tree and the Lake itself.

THE WISDOM TREE

The tree by the lake is your wisdom tree. It represents the wisdom you have gained from life up to this moment in time.

THE LAKE

The area surrounding the lake is relevant to what is affecting you as a balanced person at this moment in time and which you already know about because it is shown clearly in the picture.

When you first look at the Lake area, you are looking at the symbols which represent present time situations which are affecting your balance within you.

The lake surface whether calm or choppy is giving you the information about how you are feeling and the water itself, whether clear or not is relevant to what you can and cannot see and which is affecting your balance.

Beneath the bed of the lake will be buried past time experiences which still have an effect on you but which you have buried to try to forget.

AN ISLAND ON THE LAKE

An island would not be seen while working on the lake area and is in fact another area on the map. You will need to request seeing the island on the lake which represents your health, physical, emotional and mental.

Once you have worked on the lake, you can stand back and decide to look for the island and it will show itself. Travelling to and around the island is navigated by our thoughts.

The Island on the lake represents your health, physical, emotional and mental.

Journey to the Wisdom Tree and the Lake

1. Close your eyes and again, step onto "a" path in front of you. Walk forward past the first turning on

your left and continue until you come to the second turning on the left. Turn onto that path.

2. You become aware of a tree by the lake. Notice everything about that tree which represents you and your wisdom.

3. Now look in the direction to the lake and become aware of the whole picture presented before you, particularly noticing the surface of the lake. You can walk up to the lake and look into the water.

4. If you cannot see to the bottom of the deepest point at the bottom of the lake, request that any dirty water is removed and taken away so you can see clearly into clean water and to the bottom of the lake.

5. When you have done that, make your way back past the tree to the central path and all the way back to the beginning where you started your journey.

6. Open your eyes.

The Wisdom Tree analysis

Use the tree symbolism list found in Chapter 3 to understand what this tree is telling you about your wisdom. Also become aware of everything else about the tree, its roots, branches leaves etc.

Is it positioned where it should be as shown on the map?

Wisdom Tree Case Studies

Case Study example (1)

A client is taken to the lake area but when invited to look at the wisdom tree to the left of the lake, is unable to turn to look. They realise that their attention is drawn to another tree in the distance. Here the subconscious is helping them to recognise, by not letting them turn, that their wisdom is no longer the tree on their left, but the tree "in the wrong place".

Once you enter the map, you are in communication with that part of you and any questions can be answered.

So, on closer inspection and questioning the picture, the tree which was set to their left was dead and needed to be removed and replaced with the tree they were looking at in the distance. However, there were large stones under the dead tree which explained why that tree had died, so those stones also needed to be removed off the map. A good place to put anything unwanted is into a light in the sky which symbolically means giving what we no longer want to a higher mind, God if you like, or some intelligence greater than your conscious self. A tree planted on stones which are buried hurts cannot grow and live

It was important at this point to make sure that the new tree had all it needed to grow to its full potential which required instructing the subconscious to bring good fertile soil which would give all the nutrients the tree needed to grow to its full potential. And then the other tree was moved into place and checked that it had all it needed and felt alive.

The reason for the change of tree was relevant to the client's life experiences but also to changes they had already made on the mind map, and they understood its relevance. It was time to cast off old beliefs and move forward in understanding and wisdom.

A point to make here, is that everything on the map should be exactly in the right place according to the map and if anything is out of place, it is information to be questioned.

Case Study example (2)

The client noticed that the Wisdom Tree looked what she described as "a bit miserable". It did not look alive.

She was drawn to the roots which seemed to be above the ground as if something was beneath the tree. With X-ray vision she realised that there was a box buried under the tree.

She requested that the subconscious brought the tree to the surface and she asked her subconscious what was in it. The reply was "your sense of humour". This picture showed clearly what had happened to her and why it had an effect on her wisdom. Once the box was opened and she took back her sense of humour, the result for her was instant and she spent the rest of the day being happy and laughing.

Of course, it was then necessary to take care of the tree by giving it extra nutrients in the soil and watching the tree come alive.

Lake Surroundings Symbolism

What you see around the lake is information about what is happening in your life at the moment relevant to the feeling of balance. Every picture is information and nothing is there by mistake. Research symbols if they are not listed here.

Beach
Represents leisure or holidays.

A Building
Describing what you see as a building would probably represent your home or your working life and seeing it in this area is telling you that home or work is affecting and disturbing you.

Bulrushes
On the edges of the lake would represent protecting a new idea from destruction like hiding baby Moses in the bulrushes. Logic says that they must be in mud, so the situation is muddying the water.

Field
Analysis – This is an area of land set aside for planting crops or is a pasture for animals. It can also be used to refer to a space within which objects are visible from a particular viewpoint.
Interpretation - This represents a part of your life which you have set apart which is designated for a particular purpose and that purpose is to create something of benefit. While it is contained in its field of understanding, there is no set direction. It also represents something you wish to study usually on a natural or even spiritual level.

Grass
If the grass is fresh and cut, you will recognise that grass is always good. Its colour is healing and balancing but also

there is freedom to follow your own way forward, a new way not walked before.

Long grass
If the grass is long it would mean that you have left things undone "let the grass grow beneath your feet" and this would cause you to not see what may be lurking there. There could be stones or a snake in the grass which would represent an untrustworthy or deceitful person.

Meadow
Analysis – An open, often flat area of grass and sometimes, wild flowers, which is open to public access.
Interpretation – This gives a feeling of freedom and a connection with nature, a spiritual dimension and the God consciousness.

Mountains
These are about achievement – we climb mountains to get to the top – so they would normally represent some situation in your life which you wish to succeed at. Alternatively they could represent other people of power. People who can tower over you.

Are you climbing those mountains at the moment? Being aware of more details about the mountains might be important. For example, details about whether the mountains would cast a shadow on the lake and therefore make the lake less easy to see.

Easy to climb mountains mean exactly that, that you will climb them easily, and therefore this could be a positive which helps you feel balanced in life. But if the mountains are difficult to climb, that would be a negative. Maybe they are ice-capped, which would be telling you that the climb could be treacherous and that you would feel isolated and in the cold if and when you reach the top.

Perhaps they are grey and rocky, the grey meaning depressing and not giving you any colour in your life, and rocky meaning they are hard and difficult to climb. Or are they covered in grass which might seem a good symbol of new ways upwards (think of the movie The Sound of Music), or are there trees on the side of it, meaning that you are putting a lot of your effort and capabilities, into climbing that mountain? Remember that trees anywhere on the map are you.

If the mountains are in the distance they could be mountains you know you are going to climb, but not yet, or are those opportunities out of reach? Be aware that the information is in the detail.

Path around the lake

Where does that path go? Does it just go around the lake and nowhere else? This would represent you going round and round in circles and getting nowhere. You can use the path symbols in Chapter 2 for more information. Or is the path to allow you to see the lake from all angles, which is a benefit you have to keep you in balance.

The Sea/Ocean

The sea surrounds the map and represents the outside world. However you will only be aware of the sea in any area if it is relevant. It means that experiences outside of yourself have an effect on you.

The Sky

Check the general understanding of the sky in Chapter 1.

Sunshine

The sun is our life-giving light and warmth. If the sun is reflected on the surface of the water, it is unlikely you can see what is on the surface or beneath the water. Interpreting this would probably mean that your focus is positive and that all is good in your life. However, it is better to see the truth when it may have a profound effect on you and know that you are being affected.

Trees

Other trees besides the Wisdom tree represent aspects of you and closer inspection will give you more information why they are here in your balance area. Use the tree symbolism in Chapter 4.

Lake Surrounding Area Case Studies

Case Study example −(1)

The client was aware of an old shack by the side of the lake. This symbol represented work. His situation was that he had a beautiful home where he loved to be but his work took him to other areas in the country and although he stayed in four star hotels, the feeling he had was that he might as well have been staying in a shack. It was not like home.

As the lake area is one of the inner areas, we can remove anything which has an adverse affect on us. The point is that we are not removing the situation in our lives but the "effect on us".

Case Study example – Lake Surrounding Area (2)

In the distance, beyond the lake were a range of mountains. These were snow and ice-capped and the sun was seen beyond those mountains which cause them to cast a shadow on the lake. Mountains can be interpreted as powerful people who tower over us in life and prevent us going forward or mountains we ourselves wish to climb and represent achievements. In this clients situation they represented powerful people who prevented the client from feeling the warmth from life (the sun) and because of the snow/ice tops were cold and even ruthless in their dealings with people.

The grey shadow cast from them was causing the client to feel depressed and feeling in the dark.

The client instructed the subconscious to remove those mountains and re-landscape the whole area, creating a sun lit landscape and lake.

On and In the Lake

The ideal lake should be still and the water should be crystal clear so you can see the bottom of the lake at the deepest point. If you have ever been by a lake in this world, where the water is very still, it gives a feeling of balance.

The surface of the water in the lake is showing you what might be affecting your balance and harmony at the moment. Anything disturbing the water is disturbing you.

Ships or boats on the surface indicate situations which are causing you to feel out of balance. For instance, a rowing boat might mean that there is something in your life which you have to put a lot of effort into but with little progress.

A boat with an outboard motor is definitely going to churn you up. Sailing boats with their sales up represent a situation or situations where you may be waiting for opportunities to be given to you so you can set sail and go forward, but because they are in this area of your map, they are disturbing you.

On and In The Lake Symbolism

Ducks on the lake
Ducks represent family and usually represent you supporting them. A single swan would be a feeling of sadness and loneliness because swans mate for life and should always be seen in pairs.

Fish in the water
Fish is symbolic of hidden knowledge. Think of the fish sign for Christianity to understand its meaning. So it or they mean that knowledge which may be known or not known to you, is affecting you emotionally.

Low water
If when you first look at the water you notice that the level is low, the water must be draining somewhere. So you are being drained by some situation. Tracing where that water goes to would give you an insight into the situation.

Sharks in the water
I have often told a story of there once being two sharks in my lake. Describing someone as a shark means someone who takes from others for themselves. They are dangerous and can kill. I asked the question "what or who do they represent?" and was given the answer. Before removing

anything, we need to understand what the symbol represents. The obvious thing to realise is that they are in the wrong place. They should be in the sea, the outside world, and not in my lake. This was an added piece of information about them that they should not be in my life. Removing them to the sea would still give them a connection to my life (my map). The best thing to do here is to have them taken right away by the subconscious experts. That would certainly stop them having any affect on you.

Stones
Once you are able to see to the bottom of the lake you may see something like stones sat on the bottom, and these would represent hurts affecting you (people throwing stones and often mean people criticising you or your character or making not nice comments about you = hurtful situations).

Swimming Pool
Maybe the lake looks like a swimming pool. This would mean you are having to swim up and down, up and down, and if you don't swim and keep afloat, you might sink or drown. So this would be the situation you are in and the picture of the pool showing up where the lake should be is representing how this is affecting you.

Unclean water
Looking into the water, is it clear so you can see to the deepest point? If the water is not clear there will be a feeling of the unknown in your life which is affecting you. What might be in that water? What has caused the water to be dirty? If you come across this on your map you can instruct the subconscious experts to remove and take away

only the unclean water. Once that has been done, you can again look into the water to see if there is anything there.

In order to deal with anything at the bottom of the lake, it is best to have all the water removed. Clean water can be held on standby to be put back when work has been completed. Once the water has gone you will have a clearer view of the bottom and be able to see if there is any other work needed to be done.

The symbols of soil or mud are not a good bottom to the lake. And even sand would represent a situation relevant to leisure or holiday time which had been buried or the memory of has been buried.

We can often find some strange things at the bottom or even buried under the bottom of the lake. There may be grass (opportunity to follow a new path) or trees (you), caves (something or someone hidden) or holes (emptiness – don't try to fill a hole, they have to be removed). Sunken ships or boats would represent something you were trying to achieve sinking.

As you become aware of the symbols buried under the bottom on the lake, realise that these are all experiences from the past which affected your balance and which you have buried but which still affect you. As you view further down under the bottom of the lake you are travelling back in time, level by level.

Reflection
Whatever is reflected on the surface of the lake is informing you that you are reflecting on this subject. This

might even be your reflection meaning you are reflecting on you.

The Lake Case Studies

Case Study example (1)

This client had a ship on her lake. When asked what type of ship it was, she said "I don't know but it is very big and foreboding. So the question asked was "how did that ship get on the lake?" and it was discovered that there was an opening to the sea and the client then looked and saw that there were more ships on their way from the sea to her lake. This information meant that the situation was going to get worse.

Everything on the lake is disturbing the surface and therefore disturbing her.

This situation showed that she could not cope with life from the outside her world, but also the ships belonged to other people and so represented other people's lives affecting her.

In order to rectify this situation, it was necessary to remove the ship and close the sea entrance to the lake. Once this was done the feeling was removed.

Case Study example (2)

The client stood by the wisdom tree and looked at the lake. The water looked grey and there was movement on the surface. The client was then asked to walk up to the lake and look into the water to see if they could see the bottom of the lake at the deepest point. This they were unable to see. They were then asked to check the sky, where they saw grey clouds which were reflected on the lake. The subconscious was instructed to remove those clouds which represented other people's depressing presence in the client's life. The client then asked what was causing the movement of the lake surface and they could not see any reason for it.

It was then necessary for them to instruct the subconscious to remove just dirty or unclear water and take it right away and leave only water which was crystal clear. When this was done, they again looked into the lake water and saw two sharks swimming and it was them which were causing a disturbance in the water. The client asked who those sharks represented and they were aware of two people they had financial dealings with. Searching the internet from Sharks in a financial situation it explained that these people would be hostile to them and would make a lot of money from them and possible try to take over their business.

This all made sense to them because they had had a feeling about them. The client instructed the subconscious to remove and take away the sharks thereby creating calm within the client. This picture had forewarned them about the people they were dealing with.

Journey to the Island on the Lake

1. Close your eyes and again, step onto "a" path in front of you. Walk forward past the first turning on your left and continue until you come to the second turning on the left. Turn onto that path.

2. You become aware of a tree by the lake. Notice everything about that tree which represents you and your wisdom.

3. Now look in the direction to the lake and become aware of the whole picture together with the surface of the lake. You can walk up to the lake and look into the water. Can you see into the water and the bottom of the lake at the deepest point?

4. When you have done that, make your way back across the lake, past the tree to the central path and all the way back to the beginning where you started your journey.

5. Then become aware that there is an island on the lake which you did not see before. Travel to that island and become aware of everything you find there.

Accessing the Island

How the client gets to the lake is added information.

A boat which they have to row themselves would represent them creating a feeling of being disturbed by their health. If there is someone else rowing or driving the boat, it represents help from someone else. It may be that someone takes you to the doctors or hospital but they create a disturbance to you.

Swimming means extra effort and the possibility that they could sink or drown.

Stone Bridge – This means you have to overcome a lot of hurt and difficulties to deal with your health.

<u>Wooden Bridge</u> represents getting over a problem. A wooden bridge means you are having to put a lot of your own effort into getting over the problem.

Island Symbolism

Everything on the island is information about what is affecting your health. If not listed here look at the lists in other chapters or research.

Sometimes the picture shows your actual body and what is wrong with it.
<u>Barren</u> – Representing not being able to produce something new.

<u>Dessert Island</u> – Being deserted and left behind.

<u>Grass</u> – No set path in life perhaps. Or on a positive note it could mean that life is good.

<u>Mud</u> – Emotions causing you to feel you cannot move forward in life.

<u>Tree</u> – Use the type of tree and condition of the tree from Chapter 3. Any tree anywhere on the map is an aspect of you

<u>Wall</u> – If the wall surrounds the island, the feeling of being walled in is affecting you. Alternatively if there is a free standing wall somewhere on the island, it could represent you being limited from seeing something or moving forward.

The Healing Fountain

Although this is not normally seen immediately, you can instruct your subconscious to create a colour-healing fountain on the island. It usually comes out of the ground creating a cascade which you can step into and receive the inner healing for your mind and body.

If the fountain is like energy you will be benefiting from both physical and mental healing. The colours can be interpreted by research from the list in Chapter 15. Breathe in the energy and fill the whole of yourself with it.

If the fountain is like liquid, you will be receiving emotional healing. Again the colours in the water can be interpreted. Breathe it in and fill your body and mind.

When the healing has done its work, it will stop.

The Island Case Studies

Case Study example (1)

The client accessed the island by a bridge which they could see which was made from iron. They later discovered from a blood test they had had that they were iron deficient.

The island itself is small and the lake seems to be like a tide coming in and nearly covering it. This represented a feeling by the client of drowning emotionally but also they were suffering from water retention. From the island the instruction to the subconscious was to take some of what seemed to be the flooding waters away and re-

landscape the island. The result was that the client spent a lot of time on the toilet for the next two days and the water retention became less.

Case Study example (2)

The island itself is small and the lake seems to be like a tide coming in and nearly covering the island. This represented a feeling by the client of drowning emotionally but also they were suffering from water retention. From the island the instruction to the subconscious were to take some of what seemed to be the flooding waters away and re landscape the island. The result was that the client spent a lot of time on the toilet for the next two days as the water retention became less.

Chapter 6

TOOLS TO USE IN THE INNER AREAS

If you are like me, in life I tend to do everything myself. This was something to do with experience of expecting others to do things properly and being let down, so like many, I had the attitude that, "if a job needed doing well, do it yourself". So, until I changed that attitude on the map, I, the conscious me would decide what to create to be used on the map.?

In order to remove or alter the picture, it is necessary to use symbols for this purpose. So I requested a skip when I wanted to remove some bind weed from a tree so I could put it into it. I also removed the bind weed with my mind myself instead of instructing a worker which my subconscious would supply, to do the job. Then I looked at the full skip and realised it should not stay in the picture or it would be a part of the picture. I decided that it could fly and I sent it off instructing that it left my subconscious completely, until I requested its return, now empty again.

This worked quite well, so having now created a <u>flying skip</u>; it is readily available when it is needed.

I also created a <u>flying "drain sucker"</u>. You know, the sort of wagon that goes around the streets sucking up rubbish and dirty water from drains. I used this for the removal of any water or mud etc.

Then there is the <u>flying magnet covered in pink fly paper</u>. Now how that was thought of by me was that I had come across some people in my wood who were damaging the trees. The people were a picture of a memory of people I had come across who were destructive to you in the past. I tried to think of some way that I could remove them. The flying skip did not seem appropriate for "people", so the magnet seemed a good idea to be a vehicle to take them to the light in the sky which I saw as God and I figures that he would take care of them for me because I did not want the memory of them to continue to damage the trees which of course, are an aspect of me.?

I do believe that, while I seemed to have the idea of these tools for the job, because when on the map I am at one with my subconscious, that my subconscious would have been helping me with the ideas.

I recall going into my wood and hearing a machine and it turned out to be a wood shredder. So this represented aspects of me, not only being cut down, but also shredded. I put the shredder in the skip but then looked at the pile of shredded wood and was wondering what I could do with it. I certainly could not be made back into the trees destroyed but rather than put it in the skip, I wondered if it had a useful purpose somewhere. Immediately a <u>tipper</u>

truck turned up, not of my creation, and some men loaded the shredded wood onto the truck. I followed the filled tipper truck and it went back onto the central path and right to the top of the path to the sea where there was a ship waiting and the contents of the truck was loaded onto the ship which was in the sea (outside world). I realised that it was being taken to other people's maps as a ground covering for muddy fields. My subconscious was saying to me that I would take my experience of being destroyed to help others to overcome.

A cherry picker is quite useful if you keep finding yourself pulled close to only part of the picture so you cannot see the whole picture. Of course, this is a replay of how things were or are = being so absorbed in the details that you cannot see the whole picture. Normally just requesting a client to step back or elevate can work but sometimes it is necessary to be further away from the picture so as not to be affected by it and allowing a cherry picker, which you climb into, to take you to a safe unaffected vantage point is quite useful.

Assistance from people is possible. I call them the kingdom workers. Our subconscious is like a computer so has access to all knowledge available. Some people who cannot trust "people" are more likely to get something like angels or fairies or animals. The subconscious knows exactly who to present to you who you would trust.

If a gardener is required, one or more will turn up. Or maybe you need an engineer or a tree expert or a ground worker. Whatever is needed for the job will be there. In the next areas of your map, the Material World Areas, you might also like to request a ship or harbour expert, an estate agent or solicitor, a bank manager or financial advisor. In the material areas, this would mean that these will represent the help you need in the particular situations you are focusing on. Yes, this is a magic kingdom and it is right there inside you for you to create your reality.

YOUR MATERIAL WORLD AREAS

Harbour, Beach, Building, Garden, Village/Town.

Chapter 7

THE HARBOUR

The Harbour area is a sheltered body of water protecting the boats and ships which represent situations and projects you are moving forward or are wishing to move forward in life. The harbour is a safe haven for boats not to be disturbed by outside storms or other people's control. The size of the harbour represents the amount of time given for situations you wish to pursue and progress. Any boats or ships contained within the harbour are in your life at the moment.

Being aware of each boat or ship and its condition is information about that aspect in your life and the state it is in.

Looking out through the harbour entrance to the sea beyond shows you the outside world and how it is or can affect you relevant to what you are or might do in the future. Awareness of the sea being choppy or stormy for instance gives you the indication that whatever that outside world situation is, it may very well affect the water in your harbour and cause the boats or ships to be disturbed..

If you see a ship coming towards the harbour and you instinctively know it will enter the harbour when it reaches it, means you are seeing that there will be a future opportunity offered to you. Other boats or ships which you may see will be other people's boats and represent other peoples' projects somehow connected to you and what you do.

The Journey to the Harbour

1. Close your eyes and again, step onto "a" path in front of you. Walk forward past the first turning on your left and past the second turning on your left, and continue until you come to the top left side of the map where you will find a harbour.

2. Notice everything about that harbour and the boats or ships therein.

3. Now look out through the entrance to the harbour, to the sea beyond and become aware of the picture and any boats or ships there and their action.

4. When you have become aware of that picture, turn and make your way back onto the main central path and back to the beginning of the path.

5. Open your eyes.

The Harbour Symbolism

Big Harbour
Interpretation – Your life allows you to offer a lot of time to do the things you want to achieve.

Busy Harbour
Interpretation – You are very busy in everything you try to accomplish. You probably fill every moment of your day. If there is no space for any more boats or ships, you cannot take on any more projects even if they were presented to you.

Closed Harbour
Interpretation – If there is no entrance to your harbour there must be a restriction in your life which prevents you from taking any new opportunities or making any headway with the boats or ships in your harbour. If there are no boats or ships in your harbour, there is no opportunity for you to do anything unless you create something for yourself by building a new boat.

Industrial Harbour
Interpretation –This type of harbour is informing you that what you can or are achieving is tied into material life and situations.

Inner and Outer Harbour
Interpretation – This almost seems like two separate harbours. The one closest to you contains the boats or ships you are mostly working on but in some way, the outer harbour is more difficult to access although the boats and ships are still what you are having to work and progress with . It is just that, at the moment, you would have to

somehow move out of one set of circumstances into another.

Jetty Reaching Out into the Sea
Interpretation – Jetties are built for ships to tie up to. Those ships are still in the sea and not in your harbour and therefore are for other peoples projects which you are helping them with

Lock Gate at the entrance to the sea
Interpretation – A lock may be there to keep others out and protect what you are trying to achieve. However it could also be there to keep the water in the harbour when the tide comes out. In other words when the outside world offers you the opportunity to set sail or move forward. Any of your boats of ships which are in the harbour will be kept afloat reading for when the opportunity from the outside world offers you the possibility to go forward.

Natural Harbour
Interpretation –This harbour has been created by nature and therefore connected to natural things and is offering a natural space for whatever you wish to achieve.

No Harbour
Interpretation – You do not have any spare time or do not give any time to enjoy the things you would like to progress with. Perhaps you time is taken up by other things.

No Water in the Harbour.
Interpretation – If there are any boats or ships in your harbour but no water, you are not able to keep what they represent afloat. The opportunity is not there. Question whether the tide is out, in which case in the future you may

be able to get those boats afloat again or if the sea is so far out that it will never fill the harbour. In which case you cannot go anywhere with your project.

Quiet Harbour
Interpretation – Not much is happening in your life at the moment.

Ship Building Harbour
Interpretation – You are in the process of creating new opportunities in your life. These boats or ships will be your creation.

Small Harbour
Interpretation – You only have a small amount of time in your day to give to what you want to achieve.

Small entrance from the sea.
Interpretation – If you have a large harbour with a small entrance, it can only let small boats in or out meaning small opportunities as no big ships could enter your harbour and your life. Also any of your boats or ships which are too big to get through that small entrance, cannot "set sail" to achieve its purpose.

Stone Harbour
Interpretation – Your life will have been a struggle to be allowed to do what you want to do.

Turbulent water in the harbour
Interpretation – Find out what is causing the turbulence. Is it that there are storms in the sea area, the world, which are disturbing your water? This means outside situations are disturbing and making rocky what you are trying to

achieve. But if there is something in the water or under the water, with x-ray vision, take a look at what it is and interpret it.

Boat and Ship Symbolism

Banana Boat
Symbol – Carries bananas one way and then a cheap way to carry cargo or passengers the other way. Originally used for West Indian migrants. – Cheapest way to travel.
Interpretation – You are keeping going with this using any financial way you can find. Doing it on a shoestring.

Flat bottom boat, This type of boat would not be safe to be on the sea and is mainly used on a river or canal and sometimes needs pulling or pushing.
Interpretation – This represents something which you would not be using other than for yourself. There would be an emotional connection with it and the only way forward might be to create your own way.

Cabin Cruiser
Analysis – Pleasure craft carrying crew and passengers.
Interpretation – Something you do which involves enjoying yourself with others.

Canoe
Analysis – One person can steer with a double paddled oar. Used for moving along waterways and for racing.
Interpretation – Something you do by yourself which is personal to you and that probably has an emotional connection for you. If white water or choppy water is encountered, meaning having to deal with the choppy water of life you will be able to manoeuvre those

difficulties. Be careful not to capsize although you should be able to get back up and on course.

Cargo Ship
Analysis – A cargo ship or freighter is a merchant ship that carries cargo, goods, and materials from one port to another. Thousands of cargo carriers ply the world's seas and oceans each year, handling the bulk of international trade.

Interpretation – Things which you have or have created which will be of use to others.

Clipper
Analysis – A sailing ship which regularly took part in the tea trade from China to Britain. Speed was a clear advantage, but it also created prestige for the owners. The "Tea Race" was a national sporting event with money being gambled against a winning ship which was the first to bring the tea from China. Speed was dependant on the winds and her Captain. This type of ship gave way to steam propulsion.

Interpretation – Whatever your ship represents, it is about racing to get to the finish line before others. However, this is the first stage of this achievement and is a forerunner of something else which will be more proficient.

Container Ship
Analysis – Is a cargo ship that carries their entire load in truck-size containers, in a technique called containerization. They are a common means of commercial freight transport and now carry most seagoing non-bulk cargo.

Interpretation – Separate containment of ideas or things which eventually will be transported or will reach to different destinations.

Cruise Ship
Analysis – Luxury holiday hotel carrying people to visit and discover new places and return them home.
Interpretation – This ship is about carrying people to discover new experiences in a holiday atmosphere.

Cutter
Analysis –Various types of cutters include a sailing boat with its mast stepped further aft than a sloop, a ship's boat powered by oars or sail for carrying passengers or light cargo or a small lightly armed boat, as used in the enforcement of customs regulations and occupants who exercise official authority e.g. harbour pilots and coast guards.
Interpretation – Your ship is about cutting a way through. There will be a relevance to carry other people, the law and there is a bit of a fight for you to overcome obstacles.

Cutty Sark
Analysis – This famous sailing ship was built in 1869 on the River Leven, Dumbarton, Scotland. Because the ship was designed and built to transport tea, it is known as a tea clipper. However it actually transported a wide range of goods including wool from Australia to England. It had three masts and a square rig. It represents the pinnacle of clipper ships recording fast passage times and was the fastest ship in its day. After a murder on board and the subsequent suicide of its Captain, it was known as the "hell ship" and a cursed vessel. It can be seen today in a museum dry dock in Greenwich.
Interpretation – This is about you surviving a situation. Understand what the ship is carrying. Tea represents communication, because when we make a cup of tea, we

sit down and have a chat about something. If it is wool from a sheep, you can interpret a sheep as a follower and the wool as giving warmth relevant to that.

Discovery
Analysis – One famous ship was built in Germany and was called "World Discoverer". It was a cruise ship dedicated to explore Polar Regions. In 2000 it hit a reef and was abandoned.

Interpretation – This ship represents learning about and encountering something new for the first time. However this situation takes you into an icy area so you may feel isolated.

Dredger
Analysis – Used for gathering up bottom sediment, and disposing it in another location in order to keep waterways navigable

Interpretation –. Getting to the bottom of things which are in the way of a safe passage.

Dinghy
Analysis – This boat is often used as a ships boat for a larger vessel. If inflatable, it can be deflated and stored for another time. When inflated, it is difficult and hard work to manoeuvre with oars but easier if there is an outboard motor.

Interpretation – A project which is connected with something bigger but is difficult to manoeuvre into place.

Drifter
Analysis – Fishing boat with drift net to catch herrings. Red herring.

Interpretation – Maybe information is not of use and you are just drifting along to see what you learn. No definite direction.

Ferry
Analysis – This type of boat or ship is used for transporting people and vehicles across a short stretch of water.
Interpretation – Transporting someone else or others backwards and forwards. This might represent the need for you to support someone or others to get where they need to be. An example might be an elderly person to the doctor or some other appointment.

Fishing Boat
Analysis – A boat or ship which is for catching fish.
Interpretation – Learning, discovering and absorbing on a spiritual, mystery level, as fish are the treasures of the waters.

Galleon
Analysis – With three or more masts, used for trading or war.
Interpretation – This is an old type ship so would represent something you have been doing for quite some time. It means you trade and if necessary have to fight your way through.

Golden Hinde
Analysis – Sir Francis Drake's famous galleon, the Golden Hinde ii was used to circumnavigate the globe.
Interpretation – This boat represents being prepared for new experiences, at the same time, being prepared to fight your way through if necessary.

Gondola

Analysis – Italian boat propelled by one oarsman. This is a male world where very few women are let in and then not accepted. Moving around an ancient city built on water but it is in its dying days as the sea (the world) moves in.

Interpretation – this ship is about you helping others to cover waterways and therefore emotional travel. Italians are often an emotional culture so this might be relevant.

Gunboat

Analysis – A small fast ship with guns mounted on it, for use in shallow coastal waters and rivers

Interpretation – This boat would mean that you are prepared for a fight locally.

Houseboat

Symbol – Stationary, moored boat on water to live in.

Interpretation – Your home life is what you do. You put time and effort into it but do not really want to move from it.

Ice Breaker

Analysis – An exploration ship for polar exploration and is therefore capable of cutting through ice.

Interpretation – This represents you being in an isolated situation but able to cut through these icy times to reach your destination.

Jet Ski

Analysis – Personal water craft which is fast moving.

Interpretation – You can get where you are going quickly by yourself with this.

Junk

Analysis – A junk is a type of Chinese sailing ship. Chinese junks referred to many types of coastal or river ships. They were usually cargo ships, pleasure **boats**, or houseboats. They vary greatly in size and there are significant regional variations in the type of rig, however they all employ fully battened sails.

Interpretation – The word junk also means rubbish or old or discarded articles that are considered useless or of little value. Your hope to achieve by preparing for whatever this represents in your life and hoping that an opportunity will come along (sales) is wasting your energy and time

Kayak

Analysis – Small, propelled by a double bladed paddle so easy to manoeuvre. It is cockpit covered so that if it capsized, water is prevented entry.

Interpretation – Although you may roll over you can re-surface and keep from drowning. Seeing this may mean that if you go under you can right yourself. And you can deal with white water = emotional turmoil.

Landing Craft

Analysis – Flat bottomed boat carrying armed forces guns etc to invade another land.

Interpretation – Taking over through force. You have the ability to go into a situation which seems at first to be impossible and dangerous. There will be a fight.

Lifeboat

Analysis – Rescue boat to attend to a vessel in distress and rescue the passengers. To help those in danger at sea.

Interpretation – This boat represents you saving people from drowning or failing.

Liner

Analysis –Transporting people to another country where they will stay. Lining something ready for the next stage.

Interpretation – Carrying and supporting people to move from one set of circumstances to something new. If America is mentioned, you are forging new frontiers.

Long Boat

Analysis – the largest boat carried aboard a commercial sailing vessel

Interpretation – This represents you temporarily breaking away from something larger which you were doing in order to discover something else.

Long Ship

Analysis – Used by Vikings for trade, commerce, exploration and warfare and invaded other countries and peoples.

Interpretation – This represents you discovering and achieving what you need by whatever means.

Luxury Yacht

Analysis – This boat would be owned by someone who is wealthy. They are expensive pleasure boats.

Interpretation – You have sufficient finances and freedom to choose and allow you to go where you want to for pleasure. You invite others to join you if you wish.

Mary Celeste

Analysis – A Canadian built 100 foot, two-masted, brigantine of 282 tons. She was seen entering the Bay of Gibraltar and her crew of seven were nowhere to be seen and were never found. Arthur Conan Doyle wrote a story around that event. The boat without any crew became known as the "Ghost Ship"

Interpretation – So this represents a mystery. Why has everyone deserted you? Where did they go? You do not have the support you need to go forward with this. The meaning of Ghost Ship could be interpreted as support has died off.

Mayflower

Analysis – The Pilgrim Fathers sailed from Plymouth to relocate in America. And discovered new land and a free way of life where they could follow their beliefs.

Interpretation – This represents a new project of discovery where you will be paving your way to new frontiers and which will give you the freedom to be yourself.

Motor Boat

Analysis – A motorboat, speedboat or powerboat, is a boat that is powered by either an inboard engines or an outboard motor

Interpretation – This boat is about you going super fast forward with your feet hardly touching the ground. You may be doing this alone but may need to carry one or two other people.

Narrow boat

Analysis – A boat which originally used to carry goods along narrow, manmade canals but more often now used for pleasure.

Interpretation – There is a restriction with this boat that says you have to follow a material, world-set direction. You cannot branch out into the world with this and while you would have originally been giving what you have to offer, you then managed to enjoy the process.

Noah's Ark

Analysis – This ship was built by Noah and Inspired by God to rescue animals and family from the flood.

Interpretation – This represents something you have been doing for a long time. It is about rescuing and helping people to find their place in the world. These people will have had to deal with difficult emotional life experiences

Oil Tanker

Analysis – These are giant ships which carry oil for refining.

Interpretation –This ship is about you giving your energy and power, which you have plenty of, to help people. You are offering the foundation for them to progress. Alternatively, you have all you need to convert the energy you have to create a way forward for your future.

Paddle Steamer

Analysis – A flat bottomed boat driven by paddle wheels to propel it through river water by using steam. It is usually used for carrying passengers on short or longer journeys along a river but was also used for commercial transport

Interpretation – This represents family and friends who you put a lot of effort into helping, either by taking them on day trips or wherever they want to go.

Patrol Boat

Analysis – Naval vessel used for coastal defence.

Interpretation – You seem to be defending some situation, person or people.

Pleasure Boat

Analysis – This boat is used for carrying people for day trips in a holiday situation for pleasure.

Interpretation – This represents you organising in a holiday situation to help people enjoy themselves.

Queen Mary
Analysis – This was a floating hotel. There were two Queen Mary ships so check its name on the side of the boat. The first one started being built but work had to stop because of a depression. Later it was completed. Queen Mary II was built for transatlantic travel for the rich and famous and represented an era known for its wealth, class and style.
Interpretation – Having this as your ship means you support people to discover new ideas and reach new frontiers while you organise all they need and want. You are the queen and therefore in charge and respected by the people who follow you.

Raft
Analysis – Basic structure sometimes made from tsunami debris. It stays afloat by its natural buoyancy. It is often thought of as a vehicle to escape a desert island.
Interpretation – This situation is about you leaving behind an emotionally unfulfilled way of life. To leave that life, you have had to make do with what you have to hand and there is a sense of going into the world without direction and not being sure whether you will be lost or eventually reach a safe destination.

Regatta Boat
Analysis – A competitive boat race for fun.
Interpretation – So this boat is you racing and rushing to win the race but in a fun way.

Rowing Boat

Analysis – This type of boat has oars and is manned by one person or many, all facing backwards to the direction they are going.

Interpretation – If it is a one person rowing boat, you are putting a lot of effort into going forward very slowly. There is often the feeling of going backwards. Even then, you are not sure where you are going anyway.

Sailing Boat

Analysis – This type of boat is propelled partly or entirely by sails and therefore wind.

Interpretation – This situation is about you using whatever is at your disposal to get where you are going. If the sails are up you will be progressing at the moment but the speed is determined by what life gives you. If the sails are fastened down, you are choosing not to move forward with this at the moment.

Schooner

Analysis – A schooner is a type of sailing vessel with two or more masts and sails which is used for trades. It had speed and windward ability and often used to carry slaves or commissioned for war service.

Interpretation – This represents a situation where you can use what you are given to go forward quickly. It represents trading or exchange.

Speed Boat

Analysis – This boat is powered by an engine which allows it to be easily manoeuvred at speed.

Interpretation – You have what is necessary to achieve what this represents very quickly.

<u>Steam Boat</u> –

Analysis – These boats were known to provide commercial and passenger transport along the Mississippi River and other inland US rivers in the 19ᵗʰ century. They had the ability to travel against the current faster than other boats.

Interpretation – Because this is a river boat it can be interpreted as you having to put a lot of effort to deal with emotions of others and supporting them. You probably let off steam sometimes. Using the US would mean new frontiers and connecting two extreme points. Being a boat from the past would suggest that you have been doing this a long time

<u>Submarine</u>

Analysis – This boat is able to be on the surface of the water and go under the sea out of sight, hiding and then attacking surface ships. They can also be used for undersea archaeology and marine science.

Interpretation – This situation is about watching what is happening but not letting anyone know you are, bit like being a spy. Alternatively, you have to step into another world to discover.

<u>Tanker</u>

Analysis – An enormous ship which carries things like oil or coal. Check what is on board for the precise answer.

Interpretation – If it carries fuel, it is about energy you can offer and supply. If oil it is about having what you need to convert for many ways forward. Coal is about warmth for others which you have.

Titanic

Analysis – This ship was a passenger carrier which sank on its maiden voyage by hitting an ice-berg. Many died because it did not have enough rescue boats on board.

Interpretation – This might suggest a situation which you have not thought through. If you go ahead with this, without everything in place, this picture is talking about it not surviving. Make sure you have not missed anything.

Tug

Analysis – This is a small boat which has a great deal of power for manoeuvring other larger vessels safely towards a port by pushing or pulling them either by direct contact or with a tow line. They have to churn the water to create thrust to move or displace ships.

Interpretation – This situation is about you making sure that another or others get to where they are going safely.

Warship

Analysis – This is a ship equipped with weapons and designed to take part in warfare at sea.

Interpretation – You need this ship for the war you are having to be involved with. It may be a war of words or action but in some way it is a fight you are having.

Yacht

Analysis – A sailing or powered boat used to cruising. the circumstances.

Interpretation – If you see a powered boat, it usually means you are able to spend time going where you want to, enjoying yourself. If it is a sailing boat, then the circumstances are different, in that you have to wait for the right opportunity and depending on whether the sails are up or down.

Position of the Boats in the Harbour

Closest to you
Interpretation – At the moment these represent what you are mostly working on at the moment. Be aware of how easy or difficult it is to get on board.

At the far side of the harbour
Interpretation – While what these represent are there for you, you would have to make a special effort to board them.

Centre of the harbour
Interpretation – At the moment you are not on board. If it is anchored, this situation it represents is waiting and being held for the moment.

The Condition of the Boats and Ships

Anchored
Interpretation – This boat or ship is stationary and prevented from moving forward at the moment for whatever reason and you will not move forward until the anchor is lifted.

Broken
Interpretation – Exactly that. It represents something you have worked at which has been broken. Understand what has done that to get the full picture.

Easy to access
Interpretation – This situation is ready for you to start going forward.

Impossible to reach
Interpretation – If you cannot reach a boat, there is no way that it can be used and moved forward at the moment.

Needs painting
Interpretation – While this boat may be seaworthy and it is something you can do, it does not project to other people well and is not really ready yet.

Newly painted
Interpretation – The final touch for presenting this situation has been completed.

Partly-Built
Interpretation – This represents an ongoing project which is not finished yet.

Rusty
Interpretation – This boat or ship represents something neglected.

Sinking
Interpretation – Find out why it is sinking and what is causing it, relevant to the picture, and this will tell you the situation. If a boat is sinking it cannot survive.

Tied up
Interpretation – Being busy and occupied so not able to use.

THE SEA OUTSIDE THE ENTRANCE OF THE HARBOUR

The sea shows any effects relevant to this area of your life from the outside world. If there are storms coming, you know that your harbour water and therefore the boats in it might be disturbed but because of the protection of the harbour they are unlikely to be destroyed. Any boats or ships that you see in the sea will usually be other people's projects which are in some way connected to your life.

As I have already mentioned, if you are aware of any boats or ships coming towards your harbour with the intention of entering, you are seeing in advance, an opportunity which will come your way, as long as the harbour opening is wide enough for it to enter and there is room for it in your harbour.

Any boats or ships which leave the harbour and you see them go into the sea will no longer be a part of your life. However, the action of them preparing to go but you do not actually see them leave, is information which would mean that whatever they represent is "about to get going".

The Harbour Case Studies

Case Study example (1)

The client was only six year old. For children I describe the Mind Map as their Magic Kingdom. She described her boats as having "holes in them" which meant they were sinking. These boats represented what the child was trying to achieve, so the different school lessons. When asked why they had holes in them, she replied "because the fish have bitten them".

The symbolism of fish can be used as hidden knowledge and therefore the information was showing that she was not coping with her school work and was sinking.

I suggested that she remember that she was the ruler of her magic kingdom and that she should instruct the fish not to bite the boats and tell the kingdom workers to fix the boats. She explained that this was happening and then she decided to have the boats painted different colours and added that she would tell the workers to put gold stars all over them. I had not told her what the picture represented and she did not know.

The next day she returned home from school with a certificate of work well done and on it was a gold star. She even began to excel quickly with her school work over the next six months, much to her teachers surprise.

Case Study example - Harbour area (2)

The client had no water in the harbour and her boats were laid on their sides in the mud. On closer inspection, the reason was because the tide was out.

This picture meant that what she hoped to achieve was not possible because the world was not presenting her with an opportunity. She had the feeling that everything she was trying to do was muddied and she even had trouble keeping her ideas afloat.

The first instruction was to call the tide to come into the harbour and checked that it would stay there. This seemed possible and so *the instruction was made. The boats were checked that they were seaworthy and had everything on boat which was needed for their journey. The chains which had tied them to the side of the harbour were released.*

The changes allowed the opportunities the client had been waiting for.

Chapter 8

THE BEACH

This area represents your escape from normal, everyday life. It represents leisure and what you love to do. This includes holidays and time out. You could say, the beach represents the best escape anyone can have and "life is a beach" which means life is good or great. The sea is your connection to the outside world for these benefits.

The Journey to the Beach

1. Close your eyes and again, step onto "a" path in front of you. Walk forward past a field on your right and a meadow on your right. Continue past an exit also on the right and continue until you reach the top right hand side of the map.

2. You become aware of a beach. Go onto the beach and become aware of everything about it.

3. When you have done that, make your way back onto the main central path and all the way back to the beginning of the path.

4. Open your eyes.

The Access to the Beach

Boulders
Interpretation – A catastrophe means that you cannot go on holiday for do what you enjoy.

Cliff top with no way down
Interpretation – You do not have time to enjoy yourself.

Cliff edge
Interpretation – Danger if you try to enjoy yourself

No way to access the beach
Interpretation – If you cannot get onto the beach for any reason, you are not able to do the things you enjoy. What is the subconscious telling you which is restricting you?

Treacherous access
Interpretation – If you describe it using this word it would mean "betrayal of trust" preventing you from being able to enjoy life and do the things you love.

Steps down to the beach
Interpretation – Stepping down means you have to let someone else take over decision making to let you do what you want to do.

Beach Symbolism

Bar
Interpretation – You enjoy going out for a drink.

Beach Hut
Interpretation – You have the ability and a place to regularly go to escape.

Golden Warm Sand
Interpretation – This represents a good feeling and a precious time.

People
Interpretation – You enjoy being with other people – or have to be with other people and no people is enjoyment by yourself.

Rubbish on the beach
Interpretation – When you try to enjoy yourself or go on holiday you have to deal with other people's rubbish

Shops
Interpretation – You enjoy going shopping in your spare time

Stony beach
Interpretation – It is difficult for you to enjoy what you want to do or if you have a holiday coming up it may not be very enjoyable. Check the size of the stones and how easy or difficult they are to walk on to understand what they mean for you.

The Beach Case Studies

Case Study example (1)

The client was unable to access the beach. In her way were three big boulders. I asked her who put the boulders there and she became aware that there were a number of factors which made it impossible for her to have any time for herself.

Instructing that the boulders be taken away, which happened easily, removed those obstacles from her life.

Case Study example (2)

Similar to Case Study (1), this client could not get onto the beach and could only look down from the cliff top to the beach below. She could not see any way to reach it.

This picture represented her being so busy with the practicalities of life that she had no way of having time out or a holiday. The cliff top represented her not being able to stop working because her business was in a precarious state and could fail.

At first we talked about maybe instructing the subconscious to create an easy way down to the beach and thought about building steps in the side of the cliff. However, the "steps" meant that she could only reach her destination step by step and this would take a while, and so it was decided to reconfigure the whole picture to make the beach picture come up to the same level as where she was standing, thus removing the cliff.

Chapter 9

THE BUILDING

This represents your home or more precisely what home is to you. So while in the majority of cases it will represent where you live, it may not and could be where you feel at home most in your life.

As everything on the map is a symbol do not presume that the building is an actual copy of where you live. For example, a mobile home would represent that your home is not static and you do not have one fixed home. A static caravan would represent that you are trying to move but are not moving. Seeing the sea from the building does not mean you will live by the sea but instead, using symbolism, your home will in some way be connected with the outside world.

If your building is not on the left where it should be, it would represent that your home life is not as it should be for whatever reason.

Journey to the Building

1. Close your eyes and again, step onto "a" path in front of you. Walk forward past the field on your right and past the meadow on your right and then turn onto the next turning on the right.

2. You become aware on the left that there is a building. Look at the building and remember everything about it.

3. Now go inside the building and explore.

4. Come back out of the building to the front again.

5. Make your way back to the central path and bath to the beginning where you started your journey

6. Open your eyes.

Building Symbolism

Airport Terminal
Analysis – A place to take off to other places and return.
Interpretation – Your present accommodation is temporary and a stepping stone in preparation for moving somewhere completely different.

American Dream Home
Analysis – All you could wish for if it is in beautiful condition.

Interpretation – While this looks a perfect home, it is only a dream and not a reality.

Animal Rescue Centre
Analysis – A place to take care of unwanted animals.
Interpretation – Home to you is where animals are or unwanted people are and you have an empathy with others.

Apartment
Analysis – Multi unit dwelling
Interpretation – You may be feeling that where you life you are surrounded by people. Apart - There may be a feeling that you are separate from others or another.

Asylum
Analysis –
Interpretation –

Auction House
Analysis – Where the public sale of goods or property are sold to the highest bidder.
Interpretation – The feeling of this building is one of needing to remove or sell parts of what home is to you and of others taking what is yours.

Bank
Analysis – Where money is kept safe or where we owe money.
Interpretation – Remembering that this is a symbol, it represents what is of value to you which you feel you must keep safe.

Barn

Analysis – Large draughty building which cannot be kept warm. Agricultural building housing grain, hay, livestock etc.

Interpretation – This represents a feeling of needing to be busy, taking care of everyone and everything there. There is no warmth in the situation.

Barracks

Analysis – Military housing, dormitory style.

Interpretation – This building feels like it represents a situation where there is control by someone who gives orders and discipline or there might be trouble.

Bedsit

Analysis – Lounge and bed in one room. Cramped for living but all right to sleep there.

Interpretation – Home for you is somewhere the sit and sleep and not much more. You have only the basics of life.

Boathouse

Analysis – Is a shelter by the edge of a river, lake etc. for housing boats. Sometimes a boat which has been converted to a residence moored on water.

Interpretation – This may not actually represent a building but more that you feel at home working on a project.

Bungalow

Analysis – Single storey dwelling. Everything on one level.

Interpretation – Any building on one level would suggest that there is only one level to your home life and everything is as it is.

Cafe

Analysis – A place where people can get coffee/tea and a menu for many things to eat served to order.

Interpretation – Are you someone who serves others, making sure they have whatever they want?

Caravan

Analysis – A large enclosed vehicle, capable of being moved a car or lorry, and equipped to be lived in. The original understanding of a caravan was a group of people travelling together.

Interpretation – Your home situation is not permanent and there may be the need to move on at some time. However, you will never be alone.

Care Home

Analysis – Somewhere where someone is cared for and supported.

Interpretation – Perhaps you have to look after someone in your own home or it could be that caring for others is when you feel at home.

Castle

Analysis – This is primarily a defensive dwelling and a safe place.

Interpretation – Your home is your safe place where no one can invade your space.

Cave

Analysis – A natural created underground chamber usually found in a hillside or cliff.

Interpretation – You are at home and feel safe when you can hide away from the world. However, you barely seem to have your basic needs.

Chalet

Analysis – A type of wooden house of Swiss origin, typically low, with wide projecting eaves. A house which is used as a ski lodge, garden house etc.

Interpretation – Maybe you have one and it is where you feel most at home. Or taking the Swiss motto "One for all, all for one" which would indicate that family and friends are where you feel at home. Also because these are usually high in the mountains, this could also be used as you feeling at home when you are in a position of success.

Church

Analysis – A religious place of worship.

Interpretation – You are most at home with your belief system, sharing this with others.

Circus Tent

Analysis – An arena, where people and animals perform for the entertainment of the public. Also a place where clowns and acrobats can be found.

Interpretation – So your home must be one where you and others are performing and might even be a bit crazy there with people joking.

Clinic

Analysis – A place, in which outpatients are given medical treatment or advice

Interpretation – Either your home is a place where people come for medical help and support or you feel at home in that situation.

Converted Barn

Analysis – Once an old draftee barn, now converted into a liveable habitat.

Interpretation – Your home has certainly changed over a period of time. You have looked after everyone and now it is time for you to enjoy your home.

Community Centre

Analysis – A building used by and for the community where rooms can be rented out to groups for various uses.

Interpretation – Home to you is being part of a community. If it is actually where you live, it would represent you always welcoming people into it.

Coop

Analysis – House containing hens (females). Cooped up, cannot move or is imprisoned.

Interpretation – Is the man of the house in complete charge and you have to do as you are told?

Community Centre

Analysis – A building used by the community for social gatherings and educational activities.

Interpretation – This represents your need to be a part of a group of people to feel at home.

Cottage

Analysis – Small country dwelling.

Interpretation – A Cottage is often symbolised as a quiet way of living which is perfect for many but restrictive for some.

Court (of Justice)

Analysis – A tribunal having power to adjudicate in matters of law or what is a right or wrong. Pay court to someone or hold court which is to preside over admirers. "The ball is in your court" meaning you are obliged to make the next move and it is therefore your choice. "Laughed out of court" which means to ridicule.

Interpretation – Seeing this as your home life appears to represent a situation where someone has power over you and is judging you.

Cow Shed

Analysis – A farm building in which cows are kept when not outside or ink which they are milked.

Interpretation – Cow symbolises a woman who is stupid or annoying. And shed could be used to mean to shake off or throw away. So one might say that your home is ruled by a female whom you try to ignore.

Day Centre

Analysis – This is for Social welfare. It is a building used for day care or other welfare services for the elderly or those needing support.

Interpretation – If this represents where you live, it means you have someone or people who visit you and for you to take care of. Alternatively, you are at home when you go to meet people to support and care for them.

Detached House

Analysis – A house standing on its own and not connected to any other buildings.

Interpretation – Home separate and detached from other people allowing own space. It can mean being financially in a good position.

Drop in Centre

Analysis – Social welfare - a daycentre, which clients may attend if and when they please. It is intended mainly for people who are reluctant to be helped officially by social workers.

Interpretation – I think the analysis of this pretty much explains what this situation is.

Farmhouse

Analysis – House on a farm for a farmer and family

Interpretation –. This would represent that your work is your home and that you are the one who is feeding and taking care of everyone in your home.

Fire Station

Analysis – A building where fire fighting equipment is stationed and where firemen on duty wait to fire fight.

Interpretation – This may suggest that there is a need at the moment for you to be fire fighting which means dealing with problems as they arise rather than planning to avoid them. So dealing with arguments and anger.

Flat or Block of Flats.

Analysis – More than one home in a building. Other people living in close proximity.

Interpretation – Your home would seem to be inhabited by many people but you have your own area and space within it.

Folly

Analysis – A building with no practical purpose other than an ornament and decoration. Sometimes these are built to give peasants a job.

Interpretation – You probably don't live in what would be called your home. It is just a building for show and to keep others happy.

Fort
Analysis – A fortified enclosure, or building, or position able to be defended against an enemy. "Hold the fort" = to maintain or guard something temporarily.
Interpretation – This will represent a safe place for you to be and a feeling that outside of it there are dangers.

Fortress
Analysis – A large fort or fortified place of refuge for protection and support.
Interpretation – Your home is your refuge which allows you to keep everyone out.

Garage
Analysis – A building where a car is kept. A shop where cars are fixed.
Interpretation – Probably your home is just a stopping off place from where you can move to other places. If there is a car in the garage, you feel at home when you are travelling. If this building is for mending cars, there is a sense that your intention is to move around but at the moment you are dealing with getting everything in place to do that.

Garage with Apartment or Flat over
Analysis – Home close to car – transport.
Interpretation – Home to you is feeling free to journey to other places. Also travel is where you feel happy.

Gentleman's Residence
Analysis – A house belonging to a man or men who like things their way and there is no room for women.
Interpretation – A home of a male or males and you may be happy to have it that way or not.

Gentleman's Club
Analysis – A members only place where only men can join.
Interpretation – Definitely a male dominated place with no space for women.

Glasshouse
Analysis – A prison where everyone can see in and there is no freedom.
Interpretation – A home with a feeling of being a prison where you are watched and cannot hide.

Golf Course
Analysis – An area of land used for playing golf
Interpretation – Home to you must be on the golf course.

Greenhouse
Analysis – Made of glass, it heats up when the sun is shining and is an ideal plant growing environment protected from the elements.
Interpretation – Your home must be a perfect place for you are nurturing something which might be an idea or a thing and which you hope will grow. People who live in glass houses etc.

Hairdressers
Analysis – A place to have the hair cut, curled, coloured and arranged.

Interpretation – You may actually use your home for hairdressing and feel at home doing that or you feel at home when you are doing hairdressing

Homestead
Analysis – A house or estate and the adjoining land, buildings, etc. designated by the owner as a fixed residence and exempt under the homestead laws from seizure and forced sale for debts.
Interpretation – There is a sense with this that your home is protected and cannot be taken from you.

Hospital
Analysis – An institution for the medical, surgical, obstetric or psychiatric care and treatment of people. A repair shop for something specified
Interpretation – This could be interpreted as a feeling that you are at home helping people by dealing with their health.

Hotel
Analysis – An establishment providing accommodation, meals, and other services for travellers and tourists usually on a short term basis.
Interpretation – Your home does not appear to be your own and is only a temporary place to stay.

Houseboat
Analysis – A boat which is or can be moored on water, for use as a dwelling.
Interpretation – The foundation of your home life seems to be balanced on emotion of some kind, either steady or turbulent.

Igloo

Analysis – Temporary home made from ice but also protection from icy, cold conditions. Ice is the only thing that can be used in this environment.

Interpretation – Your home life seems to be an emotionally cold environment which you do not feel is permanent but it seems to be the only option available to you as the alternative seems to be even worse.

Inn

Analysis – A public house usually in the country and in some cases providing accommodation.

Interpretation – Temporary accommodation where you can sleep eat and drink and where there seems to be an abundance of alcohol.

Kennel

Analysis – An outside building for a dog.

Interpretation – Maybe there is a sense of always being in the dog house, so in trouble, and also where you have to be a friend and servant.

Leisure Centre

Analysis – A place for leisure activities.

Interpretation – Home is having free time or opportunity for relaxation and doing what you want which may include taking up keep fit or other sports.

Lifeboat House

Analysis – Housing for a boat used for rescuing people.

Interpretation – Home to you is being prepared to help rescue people in need and being prepared to attend an emergency situation to do that.

Lighthouse
Analysis – A place which shines a light to protect ships and people from the dangers of the rocks of life and destruction.
Interpretation – You feel at home where you can help others from being in danger of destruction.

Log Cabin
Analysis –A home while being in, or discovering, new territory.
Interpretation – You must be an innovator, discovering new experiences and that gives you feeling of being at home.

Lodge
Analysis – A small house at the entrance of an estate, originally for the gatekeeper to live. It can also be a meeting place for Masons.
Interpretation – Where you live may be a small area of a bigger place where you are allowed to live for payment and can see the comings and goings to the other part of building.

Manor House
Analysis – Medieval country house for noblemen. Lord of the lands. A residence of high standing but can be only for show. Expensive to upkeep and keep warm and requires servants.
Interpretation – So here lives a lord and/or lady who need to keep up appearances.

Mansion
Analysis – Using the word "mansion" rather than mansion house to describe the building brings to mind – "In my Father's house are many mansions".

Interpretation – Perhaps this is your perfect and last place to live because it suggests "heaven".

Mansion House
Analysis – A large, luxury home, similar to Manor House.
Interpretation – Home to you seems to be where you feel important and even helpful from a position of power.

Mental Home or Institution
Analysis – A home, hospital or institution for people who are mentally ill.
Interpretation – One suspects that your home is a bit crazy.

Mobile Home
Analysis – Static caravan used for living quarters. On wheels and is capable of being towed by a motor vehicle to another pitch if required.
Interpretation – Home is not permanent but you have all you need and if necessary, you can take all your possessions and put them somewhere new.

Motel
Analysis – A roadside hotel for motorists which has direct access from each room or chalet to a parking space or garage.
Interpretation – Your home seems to be temporary and you are ready for travelling from it.

Mobile Home
Analysis – A vehicle and combined living accommodation which can move from place to place.
Interpretation – Your home life is not set to one place and the situation you are in at the moment is not permanent.

Nursery

Analysis – A place set aside for children or plants. An establishment providing residential or day care for babies and very young children;

Interpretation – The children could be adults behaving like children. Or a place where plants, young trees etc. are grown. Anywhere serving to foster or nourish new ideas etc.

Nursing Home

Analysis – Where the elderly are nursed, similar to a hospital.

Interpretation – Your home is taking care of others.

Office

Analysis – Room or building where business is carried out. Holding Office is a person who holds a certain position or has a special duty especially one of service to the public

Interpretation – Holding a position of authority is part of your feeling at home. Alternatively you administer some sort of organisation from your home.

Pharmacist

Analysis – A place for dispensing medicines. A shop supplying all types of medicines.

Interpretation – If this is your home, you have some sort of connection with the wellbeing of others.

Remand Home

Analysis – An institute where juvenile offenders are held.

Interpretation – Is your family and or people you live with offending you?

Restaurant

Analysis – Where a variety of food is prepared and served.
Interpretation – Your job of preparing food for others is your home situation.

Rest Home

Analysis – Old people's home. A final place in life.
Interpretation – You have worked hard and now it is time for you to take the time you want or need to rest from any distractions.

School

Analysis – A place at which people receive education. A body of people, adhering to a certain set of principles, doctrines or methods. A group assembled for a common purpose. To school – to discipline or control.
Interpretation – Your role seems to be to educate others to reach a level of understanding which will help them progress in life.

Semi Detached House.

Analysis – Two houses joined together. Two homes connected.
Interpretation – There seems to be more than one family involved with what home is to you. You may seem (semi) partly detached from your home life.

Shack

Analysis – Small, usually run down building. Ramshackle. To shack up.
Interpretation – A place where you make do with a less than perfect situation. Can also mean to sleep or live together as unmarried partners.

Shed

Analysis – Simple wooden structure usually in back garden. A store. A gardener's place. To shed tears, to cast off or lose.

Interpretation – No one wants to live in a shed and nor should they. It is not a home and does not feel like one.

Shelter

Analysis – Somewhere that provides cover and protection from weather and danger etc. A refuge. A place for the homeless.

Interpretation – Not what you could call your own home but a safe place where you can stay for the moment.

Shop

Analysis – Retail sale of goods and services. Shop front showing some of what is available.

Interpretation – Your home must be used for selling something.

Skyscraper

Analysis – This is a very tall habitable building with many storeys for living, office or commercial use. Each level is a foundation for the next as if reaching for the sky.

Interpretation – While you are trying to reach for the sky and for success, the awareness of which floor you are on at the moment will give you the idea of how much further there is to go.

Stable

Analysis – A building usually consisting of stalls which is used for the housing of horses to protect them from the elements and keep them safe. The word "stable" could also mean sane and sensible; not easily upset or disturbed.

Interpretation – Using the word "stable" can mean that your home situation is stable or you feel you are not at the centre of your family and are treated like an animal.

Static Caravan
Analysis – Static = not moving. Caravan = A group of people travelling together for mutual protection.
Interpretation – If this was your building, home life is stuck although you are not on your own.

Temple
Analysis – Place of worship.
Interpretation – This might mean that home to you is your religion or ability to worship.

Tenement
Analysis – Run down block of flats in multi occupation usually for rent.
Interpretation – There may be a feeling that your home is not in perfect condition and that others who possibly live with you, are a part of the problem.

Tent
Analysis – Camping out. A portable shelter with basic needs.
Interpretation – This is not a solid base for you to live in at the moment. It is temporary and hardly gives you the bare essentials.

Terminal
Analysis – Transfer from one place to another.
Interpretation – Your home must be a temporary in between situation.

Terraced House
Analysis – A dwelling connected to other homes and community.
Interpretation – Although you have your own space, your home is connected to others

Tepee
Analysis – Temporary tent which can be transported when circumstances dictate. Used by North American Indians so they could move to better pasture when required.
Interpretation – A temporary living space which can move to a better situation.

Tower
Analysis – A tall, usually square or circular structure which is sometimes part of a larger building. It is usually built for a specific purpose e.g. a place of defence or retreat or a church tower to house a bell or a control tower. "Tower of strength"
Tarot symbol = unassailable stronghold but forces may change things.
Interpretation – There seems to be no way out if there is no door or windows and there is a feeling of falling.

Tree House
Analysis – A fun place mainly for children which is built in a tree above ground. *Interpretation* – A situation where you are the confident one holding up others and helping them be happy.

Underground Home
Analysis – A dwelling built into land or rock.
Interpretation – Going underground.

University

Analysis – An institute of higher education, with authority to award degrees. *Interpretation* –Usually, having research facilities.

Victorian House

Analysis – Old fashioned in style and nature.

Interpretation – Your home has the characteristics and ethics from the reign of Queen Victoria and therefore restrictive with little or no freedom.

Villa

Analysis – A large and usually luxurious residence standing in its own grounds. *Interpretation* – A lifestyle living of luxury.

Warehouse

Analysis – Building used by manufacturers, importers, exporters. Stored goods

Interpretation –.Are you sure you are not a hoarder or collector which makes your home hardly habitable.

Wellbeing Centre

Analysis – A place where people can receive complimentary services e.g. massage, healing, meditation etc.

Interpretation – Is home to you helping others to feel well or where you live also your business helping others?

Working Men's' Club

Analysis – This was once the watering hole for men who had physically demanding jobs. It was a man's escape from the drudgery of life. However women can now also be members

Interpretation – Home may be about a drinking place and escape after working hard.

Workshop
Analysis – A building where manufacturing or other forms of manual work are carried out. Or a building set aside for crafts. Also a group of people engaged in study or work on a creative project or subject.
Interpretation – Your home seems very hard work and you are probably always on the go with little time to relax.

Women's Institute
Analysis – A society of women who are interested in the problems of the home and interested in engaging in social activities.
Interpretation – A place where women find things to do and where they use their skills to support others.

The Outside of the building

Brick Building
Interpretation –You have build what home is to you brick by brick, step by step.

Stone Building
Interpretation –Your home has been hard to come by.

Garden at front
Interpretation –here is a sense of peace when you approach your home.

Garden at the back

Interpretation –If you have to go through the house to a garden, please realise this is not the garden which is separate from this area and this means that you have to deal with home life before you can find peace. If you reach it by going over the building you have to get over something to find peace.

Gate – A separation from the outside world which you can choose to open or close.

Hedge

Interpretation –If it is surrounding the building, you like privacy.

Fence

Interpretation –If it is a wood fence, you like privacy and make sure you get it.

Wall

Interpretation –Either you feel walled in or you prefer to keep people out of your home.

Door

Interpretation –The colour and style of the door into the building, for example a wooden door means you have created the opportunity to have a home

Windows

Interpretation –Unless it is a specific window, it represents your home being light and being able to see outside.

Roof

Interpretation – This represents how financially sound your home life is.

Wooden building

Interpretation – You have had to put a lot of yourself into achieving having a home.

The Inside of the building

Attic

Analysis – A space, or room, within the roof of a house, with some sloping walls and usually cramped height. It is at the top of the building, as far as you can go.

Interpretation – This is not a perfect situation. You are restricted and have to deal with the financial side of keeping a roof over your head.

Annex

Analysis – Living with someone else usually in a small part of their home.

Interpretation – There is a feeling that this is not your home except for a small part of it which you can make your own. Perhaps you have to live with someone else and fit in.

Basement

Analysis – A partly, or wholly underground storey of a building. The bottom or supporting part of anything. Base can mean devoid of morality, of inferior quality or value.

Interpretation – You feel hidden and are made to feel of less importance than others.

Cellar

Analysis – Underground room or storey of a building usually used for storage.

Interpretation – Are there things in your home which you try to keep out of sight, hiding things underground or ignoring? Or maybe you enjoy wine?

Dungeon

Analysis – A dark prison. An underground prison cell.

Interpretation – There must be times when you feel a prisoner in your own home.

The Building Case Studies

Case Study example (1)

The picture showed a building which the client could not access through a front door but instead felt she had to go to the back of the building where there were two hen coops.

She lived in her home with her daughter, but had allowed a boyfriend to move in with them. The picture showed quite clearly that her home no longer felt like hers and her boyfriend restricted her movements and did not allow her to have a life of her own and meet with her friends so she was cooped up.

She instructed her subconscious to remove the hen coups and make the building hers with an easy accessible front door. She changed the atmosphere by make the interior light with everything she could possibly need to feel that this was her home where she was safe and free to lead her own life with her daughter.

The result was that the boyfriend moved out.

<u>Case Study example – the Building (2)</u>

The building was seen as being quite large but when the client entered, there was only one room that she could access.

Her situation was that her mother in law had moved into her and her husband's home and she no longer felt that it was hers except for one room where she had clients to give massages to.

She decided to make the rest of the building easily accessible and changed the atmosphere with chandeliers to bring a happy, harmonious change.

Chapter 10

THE GARDEN

This area represents peace. It is about peace in your material world which in turn gives a feeling of peace within you.

Journey to the Garden

1. Close your eyes and again, step onto "a" path in front of you. Walk forward past a field on your right, then past a meadow on the right, until after those areas you come to a turning on the for you to take

2. On the left of this path is a building. Find your way behind that building where you will find a garden.

3. Go into the garden and become aware of what it is like and any specific information about it.

4. Then come away from this area, back to the front of the building and then back on to the main central path and make your way back to the beginning where you started from

5. Open your eyes.

Gardens Symbolism

Countryside
Interpretation – You find peace by going out into the countryside, close to nature.

Dead
Interpretation – What peace you had before is no longer there so you have no peace.

Flowers
Interpretation – Check Chapter 17 for the interpretation of specific flowers

Formal
Interpretation – You like everything organised in your life in order to have peace.

Large
Interpretation – It is important for you to find a lot of time to enjoy peace.

Overgrown
Interpretation – What peace you used to have has now been neglected.

Parkland

Interpretation –Parks and protected public lands are proven to improve water quality, prevent flooding and improve the quality of the air you breathe. It is a place provided for children and families to connect with nature and for outdoor recreation.

Small

Interpretation – A small garden is informing you that you only get a small amount of time and space for peace.

Unkempt

Interpretation – You have not made much effort to have peace in your life.

Walled

Interpretation – Who built the wall? If it was you it means you have to create a situation where no one can find you so you can have peace

Weeds

Interpretation – You do not make the effort to give yourself peace in the world and just let this part of your life decide what peace you can have.

Wild

Interpretation – Peace for you is letting your hair down and enjoying yourself.

The Garden Case Studies

Case Study example (1)

The garden was full of weeds and overgrown. The client did not want to stay there.

This picture represented the inability of the client to even attempt to find peace in her life.

It was decided to instruct the subconscious to send gardeners in to create a new, landscaped garden with everything to her liking and most importantly to place a comfortable chair for her to sit in.

These changes created a situation where she made time for her and her family, while surprised she was not at their beck and call, seemed to help her with the changes to her life.

Case Study example (2)

The client had a secret garden and that is how she described it. The symbolism to understand her garden can be taken from the book and film "The Secret Garden"

Her life was very controlled by others and for her to take the time to do what she wished, where she found her peace, was not allowed. Thus the story tells how the children had to slip away and not let anyone know about the garden. The client understood the information as being very relevant to her.

It was decided that nothing should be changed on the map in this area but rather she should make changes in the wood, stream and lake to change the difficulty of her life.

Chapter 11

THE VILLAGE/TOWN

This area of the mind map of your subconscious represents your working and social life. Each of the buildings represent a symbol of either of these two aspects of your life. When you first approach this area, as with all areas on the mind map, you will see "present time", and what is happening in your life right now.

Unlike the harbour area, this area represents the foundations, practical and rudimentary to your life in your world. Whereas the harbour area represents a more progressive area of your life.

You can go into the buildings if you wish to examine what happens there, in more detail.

Journey to the Village/Town

1. Close your eyes and again, step onto "a" path in front of you. Walk forward past the field on your

right and continuing past the meadow on your right until you reach a turning on the right. Take that turning and go past the building.

2. You become aware of a village or town ahead of you. Notice everything about that village/town and all the buildings. You can ask yourself and therefore your subconscious what each of the buildings represent.

3. When you have done that, turn around and make your way back past the building.

4. Turn left back onto the main central path and return to the beginning where you started the journey.

5. Open your eyes

Type of Village/Town Symbolism

Big Village – Your working and social life is quite involved and expansive.

Busy Village - represents a busy material and/or social life.

Quiet Village – Not much happening on a practical level in your life.

Small Village - Not a lot of places to visit and things to do at the moment.

Buildings Symbolism

If the type of building is not listed here, also check buildings in Chapter 9

Airport Terminal
Interpretation –Analysis – A place to take off to other places and return.

Bank
Analysis – Where money is kept safe or where we owe money.

Interpretation – Remembering that this is a symbol, it represents what is of value to you which you feel you must keep safe.

Cafe
Analysis – A place where people can get coffee/tea and a menu for many things to eat served to order.

Church
Analysis – A religious place of worship.

Interpretation – You are most at home with your belief system, sharing this with others.

Clinic
Analysis – A place, in which outpatients are given medical treatment or advice

*Interpretation –*A place where you go for medical help.

College
Analysis – An institute of higher education and learning. Providing specialized courses or teaching.

Interpretation – This represents a learning situation whether it is an actual building or it could just be something you are learning.

Community Centre
Analysis – A building used by the community for social gatherings and educational activities.
Interpretation – This could be an actual building you visit or a situation referenced to meeting others with like minds.

Cottage
Analysis – Small country dwelling. Quiet living. Perfect for some.
Interpretation – Probably somewhere you visit someone else where they have a quiet life.

Estate Agent
Analysis – A place for selling and buying houses.
Interpretation – This building is useful if you are building or selling a home or business.

Fountain
Analysis – It could be ornamental, a drinking fountain or a large central placed fountain.
Interpretation – The type of fountain might be relevant for more understanding but a fountain was often the water supply for a village which also became a meeting place. So this example would represent your ability to communicate and supply people with life giving understanding.

Hospital
Analysis – An institution for the medical, surgical, obstetric or psychiatric care and treatment of people. A repair shop for something specified

Interpretation — Are you someone who serves others on a health level?

Hotel
Analysis – A borrowed room to sleep on a short term basis.
Interpretation — Perhaps people often visit or stay with you and expect you to serve them with whatever they want.

Lake
Analysis – Lakes can be created when rain water or streams or rivers run into a depression in the land.
Interpretation — In your village or town, finding a lake would probably mean that an emotional situation has restricted your ability to work or have a social life because there cannot be buildings on that part of the land.

Office
Analysis – Room or building where business is carried out. Holding Office is a person who holds a certain position or has a special duty especially one of service to the public
Interpretation — You can think of this building as representing the administrating or foundations of something you do.

Pharmacist
Analysis – A place for dispensing medicines.
Interpretation – If this building is in your village/town, there must be a need for you to access health benefits.

Roads
Analysis – These are access ways to reach all areas.
Interpretation – Smooth or bumpy roads or pathways can be understood as easy or difficult access to buildings and situations.

Sea
Analysis – Salt water expanses between one piece of land or country and another.
Interpretation – Being aware of the sea in this area only happens if it is relevant and you're working or social life is connected with places and people outside of your life. In others words, the outside world.

Shop
Analysis – A place where goods or services are sold
Interpretation – This could be your shop window for what you are offering for sale or can represent an actual shop connection to your material life.

Stream or River
Analysis – A water way crossing land.
Interpretation – As with the Stream area in Chapter 4, this represents an emotional situation which is affecting your work or social life.

Telephone Box
Analysis – Usually these are red and made of cast iron with windows and a telephone.
Interpretation – This represents somewhere or some situation where you have to communicate with others.

Town Hall
Analysis – Office building where political and community business is dealt with. Often with a hall for public meetings.
Interpretation – This represents responsibility for the overseeing and administration for others on a practical level and keeping everything running smoothly. May also mean offering space for meetings and functions.

Treasury

Analysis –Department in charge of finance and economic strategy.

Interpretation – A store place of treasures.

The Village/Town Case Studies

Case Study example (1)

The Empire State Building was the building seen by me and it represented my technique and the building of the empire, and gave me past, present and future details regarding it. Details of my research of the building were as follows:

America = New frontiers, so something new which had not existed before.

It was built on a stream = emotion, and this represented the emotion I had put into it.

Opened coinciding with the Great Depression = Its purpose was to help people who were depressed.

World famous designed from the top down = The creation of the technique was there but then I had to build the empire which would showcase it. It had been necessary to build the foundation and structure to present the idea.

It was unrented for quite a while and did not make a profit for 29 years. = For the first 29 years from its inception, I made no money.

It was one of the Seven Wonders of the World. = I recognise the technique as something amazing for the world to see and understand.

The bottom floor has shops = *This represents my shop window for people to see the technique.*

Most of the building is offices = *The work involved and organisation involved with the technique.*

102 floors = *I checked the numerology which said it represented my soul mission and Divine Life Purpose.*

Broadcasting tower was added for TV and Radio = *Although I have been interviewed by one radio station, while writing this book, the television is yet to come.*

Airships were tethered to the building = *As you will see in Chapter 14, a hot air balloon is part of the technique.*

Case Study example (2)

A stream was seen running through the village and into an office building which meant that there was an emotional situation which was affecting the client and their ability to not be affected every time they went to work. Their work was as an office administrator.

Before removing the stream, I asked her to look at the water to see what it was like and the answer was "muddy" so on this occasion, removing the stream and its effect. But before this could be done, it was necessary to find where the stream flowed from.

When looking at the area from the ground or just above the ground, she would only be able to see that area but rising high above the picture allowed her to see the whole map and all its areas. This allowed her to see that there had been an overflow in the past in "the stream area" and she understood the memory of being overwhelmed emotionally in a previous job she had.

To correct this problem, I suggested that she looked at why her stream had overflowed and she was able to see that there were storm clouds and torrential rain which was too much water for her stream to carry.

It was necessary for her to instruct her subconscious to remove those rain clouds and excess water which the stream had carried. She saw the clouds being taken away, leaving blue sky above her stream, and the excess water in the stream being sucked away also. Then she instructed her subconscious to remove any water and mud from the overflowed stream all the way to the village and landscape where it had been.

She then came back down to the ground in the village and decided she should make the pathway to the office building easy to walk and this was her instruction to her subconscious.

The result was later experienced by her that she no longer was affected by a previous experience.

<u>Case Study example (3)</u>

This client wished to investigate why he was unhappy at work. He told me that he could not find the building he worked in but instead only saw a Telephone box. I asked what his work was and he told me that he was in telecommunications.

I interpreted his red telephone box as follows: Red = Active and busy and the size of the box meant he was confined actual or as a feeling. Although he could see out, everyone could also see him. This meant he felt or was watched and overseen by others.

Reminding him that in the material world, it is better to improve rather than remove, we discussed what he could do. If the telephone box were removed, even if he then had his subconscious build another, happier buildings, it would mean that for a period of time he would be out of work. I.E. between removing one building and before replacing it with another, there would be a time of there being no building. Time measurement in the material areas is not the same as when you make changes in the inner areas which are using instant.

In the material areas that space of no building could be a day or week or month. Therefore it was decided to instruct the subconscious to transform the telephone box into a light, bright, happy and less restricted building. As he watched, the changes happened and the process was achieved.

About two months later the client informed me that after our meeting, he had an opportunity to apply for another job for a different company which he got, and he was able to put his notice in and step immediately into the new job which he loves.

Chapter 12

TOOLS TO USE IN THE MATERIAL AREAS

The best thing I can say here is "Improve, don't remove", unless you are completely confident that you know what you are doing and what the outcome will be.

However, there are always the experts who can be called upon to advise you and help you make the improvements.

Unlike the Inner Areas where changes which are made manifest and are felt immediately within you, changes to the Material Areas on your map will happen on a different time scale. For example, if you make improvements to your building representing your home life, your home life will change at a pace relevant to the necessary interaction of the world and people. It may be that a house move is necessary to accomplish the improvements and the pieces will need to play out although at the same time those pieces will fall into place quite easily.

If as you look at the picture in any of the material areas on your map, the picture changes by itself, while the picture you first saw is present time, the changes you see are you seeing into the future.

Another example was where a client had two separate harbours, one which she liked and the other which she did not like the look of. She knew that one harbour represented her spiritual connections and achievements in the world and very separately the other harbour represented her working life. This gave her a clear realisation that if she removed the harbour she did not like, she would lose her job. It was much better to work on improving the harbour and the ships within it.

THE SPIRITUAL CONNECTIONS

Chapter 13

THE MEADOW

Here you can meet with your Spirit which is often called your higher self. It is the eternal light which you are. You only sent a part of you, who you recognise as the conscious you, to experience life on earth. This is your opportunity to reconnect. Not that you have not been connected all the time, but it is about awareness.

When you enter your light, it will give you the opportunity to speak to that amazing beautiful you and receive advise and direction. After this experience you will always be aware that your connection is just a thought away.

Once you have concluded your communication together you can then travel higher to your group soul. This will be seen as a giant light and once you enter that light, communication will again be with telepathy. Your group soul is the spirit oneness of those connected closest to you.

It will be up to you to start the conversation and ask any questions you have of your group soul.

Journey to the Meadow

1. Close your eyes and again, step onto "a" path in front of you. Walk forward past the field on the right and find the meadow next on the right.

2. Walk into the centre of the meadow and become aware that it is a bright warm sunny day.

3. Look up to the sun which cannot blind or burn you. This is your higher self, your spirit, which is pure light.

4. As you focus on the light, you will notice that it begins to move closer to you and you can now move closer to it until you can merge right into the light.

5. Unless you have a specific question, a good question to ask of the light, which is you, is "Is there anything I need to know" Allow the communication between you to be similar to talking to yourself.

6. If you wish, you can now travel higher to where you will find a larger light which is your group soul and you can merge into it. Again ask whatever questions you have.

When you have made this journey once, there is no restriction to connecting with the world of light. This can include requesting a particularly persons spirit to be in the group soul light so you can speak to them. This can be anyone who has ever lived and even the spirit of anyone still living, who you would like to speak to.

Even travelling beyond that Group Soul Light, you can experience the many aspects of God including Unconditional Love, The Oneness, The God Consciousness, and more. There are no limitations except those you give yourself.

The Meadow Case Studies

Case Study example

When the client connected with their light, their spirit informed them that they needed to pay attention to what the light was saying to them. The information they received was not relayed in words, but instead it was given in feelings and direction and was played out in the following few weeks.

Her husband was about to go on a golfing holiday and the client felt they should say to him to not overdo things and get some rest in between playing golf.

After he has left the house, the client felt that she should pack a case herself without knowing why and even though she was not going anywhere immediately.

While the husband was away and on the final day of the holiday he had a heart attack. All the client then had to do was close the case she had packed together with the money she had put with the case and her passport and travel to the country.

While the details of what was to happen were not clear to the client in the first instance, the preparation to make life easier for her was helpful for her not to be panicked.

Chapter 14

THE FIELD AND HILL

This area puts you in touch with the spirit world. Your journey in a hot air balloon helps you to raise your consciousness to meet with those on a higher vibration. There are three areas to this journey, the side of the hill, a crystal cave and the top of the hill.

THE SIDE OF THE HILL

This is your meeting place with loved ones who have passed on. It may be relatives or friends or spirit guides, helpers and teachers. You can ask for a particular person to be there or alternatively, have an open invitation so that whoever wishes to meet with you can do so. This request needs to be made before you take the journey to the hill. Communication is by telepathy, so it will be like talking in your head and receiving the answers in your head. As this world is one of free will, you will need to start the conversation and not presume that whoever is there can speak first. If I can suggest saying something like "It is so lovely to see you again" or "Why have you come" or "Who are you and what is your purpose?"

You can also request a meeting with an expert or advisor to be able to look down on your map and discuss your life from a Spiritual Point Of View.

The Journey to the Side of Hill

Before you begin this journey, think in your mind who you would like to meet from the Spirit World. It may be a deceased relative or friend or you may wish to meet your guide. Alternatively you may decide to offer an open invitation to whoever wishes to meet you and speak to you

1. Close your eyes and step onto a path in front of you.

2. Immediately on your right you will find a field.

3. Make your way into the field where there is a hot air balloon waiting for you.

4. Climb into the container at the bottom of the balloon and make sure you feel safe. There is a safety belt if you are afraid of height. When you are comfortable the balloon will start to rise and you will feel yourself going up, and up, and up, and up and then the balloon will change direction and go towards a plateau on the side of a hill where it will land safely.

5. Climb out and if you request was to meet with loved ones, they will be waiting for you.

6. It is up to your to begin the conversation. This is in the form of telepathy, where the thought transfer of what they and you are saying is all experienced in your own mind.

7. When you are ready to return, go back to the balloon and climb in and the balloon will take off from the side of the hill, back to above the field and descend until it safely lands and you can walk across the field back to the central back and back to where you started the journey into the subconscious.

The Hill Case Studies

Case Study example (1)

The client had had a very difficult relationship with her mother before she died and when she went to the side of the hill she had not asked for anyone in particular to be there but instead had given an open invitation for whoever would like to be there to meet her.

When she climbed out of the balloon she was aware of her mother who had just died and she was with her father who had died many years previously. The mother had obviously realised from the life review in the Spirit World, how much she had hurt her daughter and there on the side of the hill was able to apologise. The daughter was more than happy to accept her apology and even offered hers because she had not always been as patient as she felt she should. This allowed the beginning of a new relationship between them as they were now able to meet in different circumstances.

Case Study example (2)

The client did not feel they could go close to areas of her map because of the trauma she had had throughout her life but particularly in her early years. It was decided to go to the side of the hill to meet an expert/advisor who could discuss with her how to approach dealing with her subconscious mind map.

When she got out of her balloon she was met by someone who discussed with her changes she could easily make and together they flew down to the relevant areas.

This included the part of the wood representing when she was just 6 years old and had been abused by her father. She found the memory and the damage to the trees which had happened and removed the picture of her father and got help to heal the trees. She then went to her stream where she became aware of abuse she had received not only at her father's hands but also the men she had met throughout her life who all seemed to be of the same character.

Again, with the help of the expert, she was able to change the emotions shown in the picture. Finally she needed to go to the lake and find buried beneath it, the memories of her horrendous experiences

THE CRYSTAL CAVE

The cave is where you can meet your "Spiritual Advisor", who will be happy to answer your questions about your spiritual journey on earth. Again the question should be formed in your mind before you take the journey into the field. Remember you are still in a symbolic realm and therefore the answer will first be shown to you symbolically and then it is up to you to question what it means. The understanding will then come to you as telepathy which is mind to mind. We are all on a spiritual journey whether we realise it or not.

The Journey to the Crystal Cave

1.   Before you begin this journey make sure you have a clear question and reason in your mind.

2.   Close your eyes and step onto a path in front of you.

3.   Immediately on your right you will find a field.

4.   Make your way into the field where there is a hot air balloon waiting for you.

5.   Climb into the container at the bottom of the balloon and make sure you feel safe. There is a safety belt if you are afraid of height. When you are comfortable the balloon will start to rise and you will feel yourself going up, and up, and up, and up and then the balloon will change direction and go towards a plateau on the side of a hill where it will land safely.

6.   Find the crystal cave and you will find your spiritual advisor inside. This area is also a symbolic area, so you may first see "how things are relevant to your

question" and then by asking what it means you will begin to get the answer to your question.

7. When you are ready to return, go back to the balloon and climb in and the balloon will take off from the side of the hill, back to above the field and descend until it safely lands and you can walk across the field back to the central back and back to where you started the journey onto the mind map.

Everything you saw on your journey was a symbol and if you asked the question at the time, you should have got the answer but if not, research for the understanding.

Here is a list of some crystal symbolism which will help you to understanding the crystals in the cave and what they might have meant. They will be part of the answer from your spiritual advisor, to your question.

Crystals Symbolism

Agate
Interpretation – This crystal is a protection from stress and energy draining and also is thought to help you get through problems.

Alexandrite
Interpretation – This is considered to be a lucky stone for love and bringing good fortune. It is also recognised as a stone which brings balance between the material and spiritual.

Amber

Interpretation – This is actually a fossil which is millions of years old. It is said to ease stress and clears negative energy, including phobias and fears. Travellers often carry this stone for protection.

Amethyst

Interpretation – Often called the spiritual stone because it is thought to be the link between material and spiritual energy and psychic and spiritual wisdom

Aquamarine

Interpretation – This stone is thought to bring the energy of the sea bringing serenity and peace so a very good meditation stone. It inspires truth and letting go of stress and help with your spiritual being.

Black Tourmaline

Interpretation – Created from a volcanic eruption it is thought to heal past anger and disharmony. This stone is about keeping calm.

Blue Lace Agate

Interpretation – Considered to reduce family upsets and bring calm peace and happiness.

Blue Quartz

Interpretation – Thought to bring tranquillity relieving stress and the ability to reach out to others. It inspires hope and helps you to understand your spiritual nature.

Quartz Crystal

Interpretation – This is a powerful amplifier of thoughts. Its energy can be used to strengthen thoughts for healing and meditation.

Diamond

Interpretation – If faceted, each reflection of each facet is a truth and the whole diamond represents the whole truth. It is about being able to cut through the hardest heart and darkness bringing light.

Emerald

Interpretation – Known as the sacred stone thought to preserve love. It is considered to represent hope, prophecy, reason and wisdom.

Garnet

Interpretation – Thought to represent successful business, and make you popular. It also is used to cure depression.

Hematite

Interpretation – The North American Indians believed this stone could make them invincible in battle, protecting and healing.

Jade

Interpretation – This stone is understood to strengthen mental faculties and assist in clear reasoning. It also attracts love and money.

Jet

Interpretation – A mineral created from organic origins of decaying wood under extreme pressure. Interpreted as you having gone through unbearable pressure but now escaping that situation.

Kunzite
Interpretation – This stone symbolises being blessed with good fortune and can be a sign of new life. It releases tension and emits tranquil vibrations particularly to release a blocked heart.

Lapis Lazuli
Interpretation – Representing protection and making matters more clear. It symbolises truth and will help you become a channel for that truth.

Moonstone
Interpretation – The good fortune stone assists seeing into the future. It helps you to be intuitive and successful in love and business matters.

Peridot
Interpretation – This brings a spiritually clear mind and protects against negative emotions.

Rose Quartz
Interpretation – The love and youth stone helping inner peace and matters of the heart.

Ruby
Interpretation – This is considered to be the most powerful gem in the universe and offers contentment and peace. I can give a person the courage to reach their loving potential.

Sapphire
Interpretation – Known as the stone of destiny and the symbol of heaven and joyful devotion to God. It also can help bring about financial rewards.

Smokey Quartz
Interpretation – This can mean endurance, personal pride and joy in living. It can also help with organisational skills and the ability to get things done in the practical world.

Tigers Eye
Interpretation – Release fear and anxiety with this stone. It helps aid harmony and balance, discernment and understanding so you can take action.

Turquoise
Interpretation – Psychic sensitivity and a connection with the spirit world comes with this stone. It protects you from harm and gives strength.

The Crystal Cave Case Studies

Case Study example (1)

This lady had some questions about her spiritual journey of life. She wished to know why she was pressured by so many people to train as a teacher of Mediumship at a teaching centre in another town. She was reluctant to do this as she had a very busy life already, working as a medium and mediumship teacher in her home town.

However, after much prompting she decided to travel to the cave to meet with her Spiritual Advisor. On entering the cave she saw a bird in a cage singing and the cage door was open. She asked what this meant and the reply from her advisor was "You are singing (teaching) quite beautifully but the only people who hear you are those who come to you." He then went on to explain "We are merely suggesting to you that you fly out of the open door of the cage and don't worry about falling. The Spirit World will support you".

The client applied for the training at the teaching centre and every step of the way it was obvious that she was being helped and she succeeded to become a teacher there.

Case Study example (2)

A question was asked about spiritual choices which could be made. There were three options in this person's life and she wished to have advice from her Spiritual Advisor.

As she entered the crystal cave, her spiritual advisor was sat at a table and on the table were three cups facing down. The lady asked what he was showing her and the advisor lifted one of the cups and pointed to a nut beneath it. Covering the nut again he proceeded to move and change the places all of the cups a number of times. Then he said "which one do you think has a nut under it". Having watched carefully the interchanging of where the first cup was now placed, she said "I think it is that one". The advisor said lifted the chosen cup, "yes you are right but look there is a nut under each of the other two cups" He continued "They are all for you and even if you decide to put one of the choices in your life aside for the time being, you will come back to it. They are all for you".

THE TOP OF THE HILL

This amazing area is where you can meet with an expert to answer any questions you have about the world and the universe. Again think about the question before you make the journey. Communication will be telepathic.

The Journey to the Top of the Hill

Before you begin this journey, think in your mind what you wish to understand about the world or universe so an expert can be waiting for you to show you the answer.

1. Close your eyes and step onto a path in front of you.

2. Immediately on your right you will find a field.

3. Make your way into the field where there is a hot air balloon waiting for you.

4. Climb into the container at the bottom of the balloon and make sure you feel safe. There is a safety belt if you are afraid of height. When you are comfortable the balloon will start to rise and you will feel yourself going up, and up, and up, and up and then the balloon will change direction and go towards a plateau on the side of a hill where it will land safely.

5. Climb out and then climb from there to the top of the hill. Someone will be waiting there to answer your question.

6. It is up to you to begin the conversation. This is in the form of telepathy, where the thought transfer of what they and you are saying is all experienced in your own mind.

7. When you are ready to return, climb back down the hill to the balloon and climb in and the balloon will take off from the side of the hill, back to above the field and descend until it safely lands and you can walk across the field back to the central back and back to where you started the journey into the subconscious.

The Top of The Hill Case Studies

Case Study example (1)

I had been watching the television news a few years ago and became very concerned about the state of the world with all the wars and suffering, so I decided to go to the top of the hill to meet with an expert who could let me know if there was anything I could do to help the world.

I landed on the side of the hill and then climbed to the top of the hill, turned around and sat down, and I still don't understand how it could be, but I was sat on top of the world looking down.

The expert explained showed me dark areas of negativity on the planet but also showed me a web of light created by people like me who sent out thoughts for peace and love for mankind and the planet. As I watched, the web of light was moving closer and closer to the planet and at the same time, where the dark areas were, I saw black tar-like people, representing evil, coming to the surface and could be seen. It showed how, by using the power of our thoughts, we can all make a difference to the world.

Case Study Example (2)

This person requested to visit the planet they originally came from. When she reached the top of the hill someone was waiting for her and from there they began to travel through time and space until they reached a place she described as a different top of a hill.

She looked down onto a city which seemed to have buildings made of something like crystal and she realised this was home. There was a feeling of being homesick but at the same time she was happy that this was the beginning of a journey of understanding of who she was and where she came from and her purpose of life of earth.

Chapter 15

MAKING THE COMPLETE JOURNEY

ONCE YOU HAVE LEARNED WHAT EACH AREA
REPRESENTS BY JOURNEYING INTO EACH
AREA SEPARATELY YOUR CAN TAKE THE
WHOLE JOURNEY AND THIS IS THE ROUTE TO
TAKE

1. Always begin your visual journey at the beginning of the
central path.

2. From there, walk forward and take the first turning on
your left where you will discover the wood.

3. The next part of the journey is to walk past the wood
and to the very end of that path where you will discover a
stream or river etc.

4. Return along that same path, back past the wood, to the
main central path and turn left.

5. Take the next turning on the left to a tree by the lake.

6. Then return to the main central path again and turn left and make your way to the very top of the path on the left where the harbour is.

7. Travel along the coast to the top right, where there is a beach.

8. Return back along the main central path and take a left turn along a path where you will find a building.

9. Behind the building there is a garden to discover.

10. Come back to the front of the building and continue along this path to the village or town.

11. Return along that same path, past the building to the main central path and back to the beginning before you open your eyes.

12. The meadow and field can both be accessed from the main central path in whichever order you wish.

It is important not to cross from one part of the map to the other but to always follow the route as explained above. Otherwise any journeying in and from each area means you are still in that area.

Chapter 16

COLOUR SYMBOLISM

BLACK - *(Not a colour but is absence of light):*
It represents a deep melancholy feeling and not being able
to see any good in anything. Also could be bitterness and a
desire for revenge. Despondent.

BLUES *(Communication and Truth):*

Black Blue – Muddled thinking and confusion. Angry and
speaking harshly.

Bright Blue – Religious feelings and devotion, spirituality,
loyalty, truth, trustworthy, uplifting and clear
communication. It can mean a sensitive person who is easily
hurt.

Brown Blue – The Blues and depression. Opportunity to
achieve and excel is stifled.

Navy Blue – it indicates an in-pouring of information from a deep pool of knowledge. It could be levels of intuition sometimes strong but often unconscious. Represents business or psychic people.

Royal Blue – High thoughts and words. Purposeful knowledge and communication. For healing - reduces trauma from an accident or illness.

Sky Blue – Trying to reach for the sky and achieve but nothing yet of substance. Perhaps communication is a bit airy fairy. This colour may be a feeling of being left out, of a cool situation where communication is not as good as it might be. Lack of attachment to knowledge.

Turquoise – New Age Colour. Going through or hungry for knowledge and understanding of life. Obsessive spiritual growth, cannot get enough information.

BROWNS *(Opportunity)*:

Golden Brown – Industriousness and ability to organise. Opportunity.

Muddy Brown – Overly materialistic, selfish personality. Avarice.

Rich Chocolate Brown – Denotes an affinity with the earth.

<u>GREENS</u> *(Balance and Healing)*:

<u>Bottle Green</u> – Not feeling well. Life pulling one down.

<u>Bright Green</u> – Shows a balanced person capable of being a social or welfare worker. They have compassion and admired.

<u>Dark Silver Green</u> – colour of pine needles is recovery from nerves and stress. Not able to help others.

<u>Emerald Green</u> – Balance gained from understanding life and its purpose. Ultimate knowledge.

<u>Grass Green</u> – Clear and bright suggests storms have passed and growth and renewal are happening

<u>Lime Green</u> – Jealous, possessive feelings. Lower intellectual and critical faculty.

<u>Muddy Ugly Dark Green</u> – Shows envy or jealousy.

<u>Pastel Green</u> - Represents a peacefully evolving process. Working towards balance and healing

<u>Pea Green</u> – Envy.

<u>Peacock Green</u> – Green with a hint of blue represents an intuitive growing process.

<u>Sickly Lemon Green</u> – Seen above the heads of people lying to you or being deceitful

Spring Green – New growth. A healing colour that helps stimulates the regeneration of injured tissues. It generates a natural healing process. Not to be used on cancer.

GREY - *(Depression):*

All Greys – Suffocating energy. A narrowly focused mind, which is tightly closed and locked. Conventional and lack of imagination. Outwardly cold and hard, sometimes friendless. Depression.

Grey with Red Flecks – *(Anger)*

LIGHT - *(Illumination)*
Connected to higher minds and the God consciousness, higher thoughts and goals.

ORANGES *(Care)*

Bright Orange – Made up of red (the physical) and yellow (the mental). Balancing and harmonising. A transitional colour. Anticipation can be magnetic personality.

Dirty Orange – Intellect used for selfish ends, prize and ambition.

Muddy Orange – Laziness or repressing something.

Orange to Green – Recovering from illness.

Strong Orange/Brown – Vigilance. Dealing with emotion.

PURPLES: *(Ego)*

Amethyst – Truthful, cannot tell a lie.

Lavender – Mixture of violet and white. Master entity is working with the subject.

Lilac – Person who has failed, trying to live up to the something, but failing. However on a positive note is beginning a journey of self worth.

Indigo - Intuitive and spiritual. Reaching for spiritual understanding. Not afraid to ask and seek knowledge. Also sharing the knowledge gained.

Purple – Reached a level of confidence in one's own ability.

Violet – A mixture of dark blue of unlimited knowledge with bright red of activity – Activated unlimited knowledge.

REDS: *(Action)*

Black/Red – Force and angry determination in action.

Crimson – Christ consciousness, love, sacrificial, perfect love.

Bright Red – Willpower, strength, determination, energy.
Actively moving forward.
Fighters who will get to the top.

Dark Red – Temper. Hatred of tolerance.

<u>Deep Red</u> – Purpose Realised. Deep love.

<u>Dirty Red</u> – Passion and sensuality.

<u>Light Red</u> – Lacks willpower or has a complex.

<u>Pink/Red</u> – Love in Action. Caring

<u>Pink</u> – Loving nature. Giving and Receiving. Check which red. If highest form of red mixed with white this is universal love.

<u>Pink/Red</u> – Love in Action. Caring

<u>Pale Washy Pink</u> – Insecure in love

<u>Ruby Red</u> – Go, go, charge. *(Also see ruby in Crystal Symbolism in Chapter 12)*

<u>Scarlet</u> – Power, strength, courage.

<u>SILVER</u> – *(Service)*.
Serving others and humanity. Not only caring but also acting. Dedication.

<u>WHITE</u> – *(Reflection)*
It is an achromatic colour that reflects all visible light of the spectrum and is the absolute presence of light. It is the highest colour and attainment.

YELLOWS: *(Mind)*

All Yellows – represent intellect and conscious mental involvement, studying and learning.

Bright Yellow – Joy and brightness. A sunshine feeling.

Dirty Yellow – Intolerant, craftiness. Person who thinks everything is wrong. Negative thoughts.

Gold – Wisdom, knowledgeable speaker. Will definitely make contact with the Spiritual World. Spiritual growth. It is also of use as a protector, cleanser and purifier.

Lemon – Highest type of intellectual activity.

Light Yellow – Thoughts still forming.

Chapter 17

ANIMAL SYMBOLS

<u>Animals seen anywhere on the map represent
characteristics or situations relevant to you or others.</u>

<u>Ant</u>
Analysis – Small social insect which lives in a colony and is
group minded. It is industrious, persevering, and step by
step with group effort and teamwork achieves it aims. It is
able to carry much larger objects than itself, like a leaf etc.
A queen ant has wings and is able to fly until it falls
pregnant and then tears off its wings, sacrificing the ability
to fly for the birth of its new-born.
Interpretation – Seeing an ant or ants represent working
together in co-operation with and for others to achieve a
group aim. Seeing a flying ant represents sacrifice for child
or children.

<u>Badger</u>
Analysis – Fat, short legged with poor eyesight, these live
underground in burrows which may be extensive. Some are

solitary while others form clans of between two and fifteen. They can be vicious and attack with powerful aggression and will even fight to the death.

Interpretation – This symbolises someone who is fearless and bold and quick to express their feelings. Whoever this animal is representing, they fight for what they want and push ahead in life. They may be solitary or part of a small group.

Bat

Analysis – There are many species of bat with widely diverse traits. There are large bats which live on fruit and get around visually and there are small bats which mainly feed on insects which use their amazing auditory perception and built in sonar to navigate in the dark as it is a night creature. They are very sociable hanging close together.

Interpretation – In North American symbolism it is understood as signifying that transformation of the ego self is happening, the end of a way of life and the start of another. Although a little frightening, there is a need to grow spiritually and trust. It is a time to let go of old habits and although you seem in the dark, know that you will find your way. You will master intuitive and clairaudient abilities. There will be opportunities to meet and mix with many people. Don't worry if people think you are a bit batty.

Bear

Analysis – Normally the bear is a gentle giant but it can rise up and fight when necessary and particularly to protect its family. The most dangerous animal is a bear mother protecting her cubs. She gives birth in her sleep. Bears hibernate in the winter months.

Interpretation – It indicates a time for introspection, for looking within, for seeking truth. Seeing bear shows that the answers are all within you. You may need to defend those you care for or something which is important to you. The Celtic tradition holds that bear is a fierce protector and highly sought after guide so it represents giving understanding to others.

Bee

Analysis – These are communal and social creatures and each knows their place within the system. There is one queen bee and others are worker bees and drones. Known which type of bee you saw. Worker bees are known for their role in pollination and for producing honey and beeswax. Drones are unable to sting and have one function which is mating with the queen and continuing the propagation of the hive.

Interpretation – This may represent someone being very busy, industrious and cooperative as part of a team, producing something special like the honey of life, for the benefit of a community

Beetle

Analysis – Beetles have a hard armoured shell and some have lost the ability to fly. They undergo a metamorphosis of a series of abrupt changes to their body structure.

Interpretation – In ancient culture symbolism they were believed to address issues in both the terrestrial and celestial worlds. Seeing a beetle may mean that you are at a crossroads where there is a choice of continuing on the same path or breaking free and completely changing your life to be enlightened.

Birds

Analysis – A creature which can fly and communicates visually and through song. They build their nests when the time is right to have their young and sit on the eggs to keep them warm and for incubation. When the eggs hatch they feed their young until they can fly.

Interpretation – Seeing a bird suggests the ability to fly and see from a bird's eye view. Hearing birds or a bird is about communication, so receiving some information.

Blackbird

Analysis – They defend their territory and can be aggressive in the spring when they compete with others for good nesting territory. They can fly hundreds of kilometres.

Interpretation – There is a song "Blackbird singing in the dead of night, take these broken wings and learn to fly. All your life, you were only waiting for this moment to arise". This may be the message from seeing this bird and it gives you the knowledge that you can recover from hurt and vulnerability and travel and succeed further than you think.

Bluebird

Analysis – An American bird which is territorial and prefers open grassland and scattered trees.

Interpretation – Songs about this bird are "There'll be bluebirds over the white cliffs of Dover, tomorrow, just you wait and see" and "Somewhere over the rainbow bluebirds fly". Both seemingly impossible and yet there is a message with seeing this bird that the dream of new things and freedom after difficulties is possible if you.

Butterfly

Analysis – A flying insect with brightly coloured wings. It has a life cycle which consists of four parts; egg, larva, pupa and adult.

Interpretation – Seeing a butterfly means that you have gone through a transformation where once you saw the world from a small vantage point but now you are flying and seeing the world from a very different perspective. In Chinese culture, seeing two butterflies together symbolises love.

Cat

Analysis – Cats are independent animals commonly kept as pets. They can be loving, particularly to humans, but it is also a killer who can stealthily bate their prey. There is a saying that a cat owns your home but you pay the mortgage.

Interpretation – Seeing a cat either representing you or someone else would indicate two sides to the person. While very loving, you or they are capable of turning suddenly without any warning to destroy.

Chicken

Analysis – A female domestic bird which lives communally for the incubation of eggs and raising their young. There is a pecking order and if one is removed this causes a temporary disruption to the social order. In some cultures, chickens are sacrificed.

Interpretation – There a need to live with others and depending who is in charge, may find themselves subservient to another or others. It may be that you need to be brave enough to face and deal with a difficult situation. Do not allow yourself to be sacrificed by someone.

Cow

Analysis – A cow is a large livestock animal kept for milk or meat and is often a docile creature which easily directed and controlled, but can be dangerous and attack. In Hindu tradition they are to be treated with the same respect as one's mother.

Interpretation – Seeing a cow can mean being subservient and there for others. It can also represent a mother figure who needs respect or might attack.

Crab

Analysis – Crabs generally live in salt water but can sometimes be found in fresh water and on land. They have a hard shell and two claws. They typically walk sideways as this is more efficient for them. They communicate by drumming or waving their pincers and can be aggressive towards each other. However, they have been known to work together to provide food and protection for their family.

Interpretation – See a crab can indicate someone who is self protective and sometimes retreat when hurt but can attack if necessary. However they are sensitive inside. Whatever they are trying to achieve, they never deal with in a direct way but instead go round the subject, still reaching their destination they were aiming for.

Crow

Analysis – A black bird known to fly the straightest and shortest way to where it is going, which explains the saying "as the crow flies". It makes a sound like "caw" and a baby saying caw expresses pleasure. It is considered to be one of the most intelligent of creates, is an adaptable and opportunist species. North American Indian cultures knew is as a shape shifter.

Interpretation – This bird represents a direct speaker with a powerful voice to deal with what seems to be out of harmony, balance or are unjust. It may suggest that it is time to speak your truth, live your truth and know your life's mission. It is about have many sides to oneself and the ability to wear many hats and if necessary become a master of illusion.

Deer

Analysis – A deer is a timid and gentle, caring, mothering, intelligent and watchful creature who is aware of danger and protects itself by hiding during the day. It dwells either in forest or plains along with other deer. The North American Indians knew it for touching the hearts of all wounded beings and showed unconditional love that asks nothing of others, not even that they change

Interpretation – Seeing a deer on the map represents someone who, while appearing timid and fearful, is prepared to be caring and supportive of others, while at the same time being aware of dangers.

Dog

Analysis – This is a pack animal which has a deep sense of service, loyalty and obedience to its master or pack leader. It can be a pet or guard dog and has the potential to be trained as a guide dog, hunting dog or sniffer dog.

Interpretation – This represents someone who has a profound sense of duty, will never let you down and is the most loyal of friends and companions. The first to speak out against injustice, they will always defend their loved one. Hindu belief is that they guard the doors of heaven and hell.

Dolphin

Analysis – A sea animal known mainly for being friendly with a unique relationship with humans, even saving them from disaster. They communicate with a rich and varied set of sounds and experiments have proved they can share information telepathically.

Interpretation – Seeing dolphin is about the ability to communicate and be a link to some solution for people. By learning how to change the rate or rhythm of energy within, you can tap into all levels of consciousness. It represents being more evolved.

Dove

Analysis – Like the pigeon this is a stout bodied, but white bird which feeds on seeds, fruit and plants. . In Christianity, a dove was released after the flood to find land and returned with an olive branch to let Noah know that there was land

Interpretation – This symbol is recognised as peace, motherhood and care. It is about finding the solution of life itself and may be a message from spirit.

Dragonfly

Analysis – An insect with large eyes, an elongated body and two pairs of transparent wings. It is often seen flying over water.

Interpretation – This can represent the winds of change, the messages of wisdom and enlightenment and communication from the elemental world. It may be time to break down the illusions which have held you back, restricting your actions or ideas. It can be an opportunity to take the pathway of transformation by applying the art of illusion to your present situation.

Duck

Analysis – A waterfowl most often seen with its mate and family orientated. It is territorial and determined to fight to protect its family and keep its mate.

Interpretation – Seeing ducks represents family. It could be about avoiding something.

Eagle

Analysis – A large bird that can fly to great heights, usually alone, and it often makes it home high in the mountains. They fly above any storms and even use the storm to lift up higher. They also have accurate eyesight. Its sharp, gripping talons can symbolised as removing all evildoers

Interpretation – Although family is important, you often find yourself alone as you work to reach great understanding and knowledge, particularly of a spiritual nature and will always complete by overcoming all obstacles. Connecting earth and heaven, and also often symbolised as men of action occupying high and weighty affairs, it has the capacity to deal with all evil.

Fish

Analysis – Aquatic vertebrates of various types and sizes which live in water.

Interpretation – Hidden knowledge and secrets of the world because they live in a different existence from our own.

Frog

Analysis – A cold blooded, four-footed land and water creature which can leap long distances. They live a solitary life in damp places. A frog can also be seen as unclean and a plague upon one's house.

Interpretation – Perhaps seeing a frog indicates someone emotionally hiding away and being an ugly nuisance. Is it time to clear off feeling tired and muddy?

Geese

Analysis – When these birds fly, they fly in formation and the thrust of their wings creates uplift for the whole flock which adds a great flying range. If one goose falls out of formation they will have more difficulty in keeping up the pace. Also if one goose is shot or hurt and falls to the ground, it is usual for two other geese to accompany them and stay with them until they die, then catching up with the flock or joining another passing flock of geese. The lead goose relocates into the formation when it is becoming tired and another goose takes its place as the leader. When a goose is on the ground they look cumbersome, thus the saying "silly goose".

Interpretation — If you see them flying, this is about sharing a common direction and the need to work together with others to achieve your aims and destiny in life, sharing leadership when required and supporting each other as they continue working towards the same aims. On the ground, there will be a feeling of not being in the right place and a need to fly with others of like mind.

Goldfish

Analysis – A small member of the carp family, this is a fish now used for ornamental purposes which is kept mainly in aquariums or ponds.

Interpretation – Wisdom and abundance and wealth through precious knowledge gained. This represents good luck and good fortune which can be shared.

Hen

Analysis – A female chicken, other poultry or game bird.

Interpretation – Fussing like a mother hen is a saying about someone who is motherly and fusses. Hen is slang for woman and it can symbolise love, safety, security, nurturing and self sacrifice. This represents an excellent teacher to their family but when the children are ready. The mother uses tough love and leaves them to sink or swim.

Horse

Analysis – A horse can be a servant of carrying you, transporting you and working for you. There are many breeds and types of horses including stallions and cart horses. They have a strong fight or flight response and have acute senses and are aware of their surroundings at all times. Also they are naturally herd animals and do not like to be isolated.

Interpretation – First know what type of horse it is that you see and what it purpose would be in our world. Is it about climbing on its back and feel the freedom of running in the wind or being taken to show you something.

Insects

Analysis – there are more than a million described species of insects and they represent more than half of all known organisms.

Interpretation — These represent a master of details; too busy getting on with their own business to notice anything else. Seeing these suggests a situation of others being pests or parasites.

Koi Fish

Analysis – These are ornamental fish which can live between 50 and 75 years and have even been recorded to have lived to 200 years. They were given as a gift by a Chinese King to Confucius

Interpretation — As all fish are hidden knowledge, seeing koi might represent an understanding of philosophy and great achievement which will last.

Magpie

Analysis – Long tailed bird with black and white plumage are known for their noisy chattering. It is one of the few birds to recognise itself in a mirror. They are also scavengers, predators and pest destroyers

Interpretation — These represent happiness and a jovial approach to life yet can be a shaky personality as they represent unpredictable behaviour or situations around you. Magpies like shiny things and so are drawn to trying to attain them in whatever manner or behaviour they can. You can also use the rhyme – One for Silver, Two for Gold, Three for a secret never to be told.

Mole

Analysis – A small burrowing mammal with dark velvety fur, a long muzzle and very small eyes which feeds mainly on worms and grubs.

Interpretation — A mole is also a spy which goes underground but then pretends to be a friend. They are actually the enemy.

Monkey

Analysis – This is a non human primate often considered to be a close relative of humans.

Interpretation — This represents the character of a mischievous child and this may represent trickery. The Chinese horoscope meaning is of an intelligent person with keenness of mind but with a superiority complex which often has a low opinion of others. It cannot live without movement and hates to be excluded, ignored or have its self-confidence shaken. They can be adaptable to any situation but their moods can change in an instant. They love to talk.

Mouse
Analysis – A small rodent found living in houses or in the fields. They hide in holes and burrows.
Interpretation — These represent seeing up close and paying attention to details. It is about scrutinising everything. They can represent being fearful of life and only see a big lump of cheese and not the mousetrap.

Owl
Analysis – An owl is a night bird, hunting for its prey at night. It can turn its head to see everything around them.
Interpretation — An owl is symbolically linked with Clairvoyance, astral projection and magic. This is about being able to see in the dark which gives great advantage because it cannot be deceived. It knows more about an individual's inner life than that person knows themselves. This is the understanding of enlightenment.

Parrot
Analysis – A brightly coloured bird which lives in the wild but is also a pet bird kept in cages. It has the ability to copy and repeat words and sounds.
Interpretation — These are symbolic of a flamboyant personality which lacks a personality of their own and is dependent on others for views, opinions and ideas. It could represent someone who is copying you or your work.

Peacock
Analysis – The male is a beautiful bird which sprays out its feathers creating the most beautiful display to attract.
Interpretation — Seeing peacock represents displaying beauty – showing off.

Phoenix
Analysis – This is a mythical bird dating back to ancient civilizations. At the end of its life, it was believed to create a pyre of twigs and ignite itself. It then burns to ashes and then rises from the ashes to live another thousand years. During its life, it did not get sick or afflicted by disease.
Interpretation — Seeing a phoenix could be a sign of bouncing back from adversity and triumphing against all odds and the impossible. It can mean spiritual rebirth or transformation.

Pig
Analysis – A farm animal noted for living in dirty or untidy conditions
Interpretation — The saying pig headed means foolish or stubborn and another saying "eating like a pig" is a messy or disgusting eater.

Pigeon
Analysis – A bird which dwells mainly in cities and feeds off the life of the urban society. Accepting food from humans and pecking at dropped crumbs. There are also homing pigeons and wherever they are taken they will always find their way home.
Interpretation — If you see a pigeon you may be in a situation where you have to find your way home or where you belong. At the moment they may represent relying on others for all your needs and having to fit into the situation.

Pike

Analysis – This is a predatory fish with a torpedo-like shape and sharp pointed head and sharp teeth. They have stripes along their back providing camouflage among weeds. They feed on smaller shoal fish and even smaller member of their own species and anything which comes into their water. Russian mythology says that if you catch a pike and then release it, it will grant a wish.

Interpretation – As all fish are representing hidden knowledge, seeing this one would mean that this situation is not what it seems and it is a dangerous situation. Maybe someone close will destroy a person or situation.

Rabbit

Analysis – Rabbits are a small, long eared burrowing animals which live in groups and are not found on their own.

Interpretation – This represents being fearful and not wanting to be far from home. It also is happiest with others company. The saying breeding like rabbits could mean being industrious producing something.

Rat

Analysis – A gnawing animal larger than a mouse which will attack if cornered. It lives anywhere hidden including in sewers.

Interpretation – This can represent being ratted on. In other words, someone who discloses your secrets, or tells untruths about you. Rats will desert a sinking ship so will not stay around to help you.

Raven

Analysis – A bird of prey of the crow family. Famously they are called "guardians of the tower of London". The story goes that there must always be 6 ravens in the tower ground or the kingdom will fall. They always have a seventh in reserve for this reason.

Interpretation – Seeing this bird represents mystery, magic and guarding something precious (crown jewels). It is the power of the unknown as it is the colour of the void, the end of something unless its magic is used.

Robin

Analysis – Called Robin Redbreast, this bird is most often seen in the winter and has come to represent Christmas. It is territorial to the death. Like the nightingale it will sing through the night. It is known to sometimes feed other birds chicks.

Interpretation – Seeing robin can be the beginning of something special even though life has seemed at a standstill. It is time to share your knowledge with others.

Salmon

Analysis – These fish spend their entire life in the ocean but return to their home stream or river and swim upstream against the currents to spawn. They expend all their energy swimming against the currents and digging the nest in the stones of the river bed and then dies and is eaten by other animals.

Interpretation – This fish represents a life of experience in the world and then hard work to get to the point where you can share your knowledge and ideas. This seems to be the purpose of your life.

Seagull

Analysis – This is a large sea bird which spends part of the year on land and part at sea. They live in colonies and can be aggressive and a scavenger when on land. They are noisy having a loud call.

Interpretation – Seeing this bird represents someone who is loud and sometimes aggressive. They will take what they want any in any way they want. They lack concern for life and things and can be a nuisance. Be careful or they will steal your food from your mouth.

Sheep

Analysis – A farm animal used for wool from its coat and meat. In Christianity the lamb was sacrificed for the good of others.

Interpretation – This may represent following the sheep or leader, even into danger, unless you are a black sheep, in which case you will be independent.

Shark

Analysis – Various and many marine fish. They can often be seen before they attack by the dorsal fin showing above the water.

Interpretation – This has a superior authority and is a master of survival. It takes opportunity, meeting life full on. There are dangers in dealing with people the shark represents as they are rapacious crafty people who take advantage of others, often by using them.

Snake or Serpent

Analysis – A long creature that slithers along with no legs and some can swallow large prey whole. It has a scaly body and fused eyelids and many are poisonous.

Interpretation – Seeing a snake may be indicating living through many snake bites and the need to transmute poison. They may represent a snake in the grass situation where there is an untrustworthy or deceitful person. If described as a serpent, think of the story of the Garden of Eden and temptation.

Sparrow

Analysis – The house sparrow is the most common sparrows. They nest on buildings and stay with their mate for life. They are fast, noisy and gregarious social creatures and live in colonies.

Interpretation – Birds often represent communication and seeing a sparrow would normally symbolise domesticity and being a competent home maker. It is said that God knows even when a sparrow falls so can be a symbol of divine providence, freedom and love.

Spider

Analysis –An eight legged insect which spins a web to catch its prey.

Interpretation – Be careful of who or what the spider represents on your map. It can mean coming too close to an entangled situation and be aware of what the web represents because if you go too close you will never escape.

Squirrel

Analysis – Known as the tree rat they have are able to dart this way and that with speed. They busy themselves by collecting and burying nuts while there are plenty, in preparing for the winter time of scarcity.

Interpretation – Seeing this is about being prepared for the future perhaps keeping a little money aside ready for change or putting aside thoughts and information for later.

Stork

Analysis – A large, long legged, long necked wading bird with a long stout bill. They cannot make any calling sound but instead clatter their bills to make a noise. They conserve energy when flying by gliding. They live in flocks of sometimes 40 or 50 and migrate in an orderly fashion.

Interpretation – This bird in folklore carries a baby and therefore is the bringer of new life and new beginnings. It symbolises a creative and speculative individual and also refers to birth and rejuvenation. As they are models of parental devotion, so seeing this bird signifies that you take care of what you have cultivated in thought or creation. They bring luck and harmony with them.

Toad

Analysis – An amphibian which can live for 40 years. It looks like a frog but has a drier bumpy skin which allows them to blend into its surroundings, and lives more on land than in water. Most predators do not like the taste of them.

Interpretation – This is traditionally a negative symbol, commonly viewed as a demonic creature. We use the term of calling someone a toad as meaning a loathsome person.

Tortoise

Analysis – A slow moving, land animal with a heavy dome shaped shell and clawed limbs. They can live for 150 years or even more.

Interpretation – Seeing a tortoise represents long and slow progress but ultimately, like the story of the hair and the tortoise, the race will be won. It is difficult to walk forward in life but perseverance and focus on the end result means you will achieve your desire. The shell represents the ability to be protected in your home and when you choose, no one can penetrate your thoughts and ideas or even your attention.

Trout
Analysis – Normally a fresh water fish whose colour creates a camouflage based on its surroundings. However, the Rainbow Trout can spend 2 or 3 years at sea before returning to fresh water.
Interpretation – Seeing a rainbow trout can be about being flamboyant and successful in business. Another fish representing hidden knowledge but that knowledge when it comes to light may bring a sudden unexpected surprise.

Unicorn
Analysis – An ancient legendary, white horse-like animal with one horn in the centre of its head. It has been mentioned throughout ancient history and is even in the bible. A symbol of purity and grace, it is said that only a gentle virgin maiden can tame the unicorn.
Interpretation – Seeing a unicorn is a symbol of mystery which is difficult to capture. It is known for healing magic and to see one is to have a wish granted if you are able to capture it.

Vulture
Analysis – A very large bird of prey with broad wings, a bald head and soaring flight. It is a scavenger, feeding on carcasses, seldom attacking healthy animals. They gorge themselves when food is plentiful and the composition of their stomach enables them to be able to clean up meat which may be diseased, preventing decay and disease so is

known as nature's disposal unit. Two dots on their front change from blue/grey to red when they are angry.

Interpretation – Seeing a vulture refers to a greedy individual who preys greedily and ruthlessly and looks for opportunities to take whatever it wants when the time is right. It is also a symbol of cleaning up at the end of something and getting rid of the aftermath. Whoever this represents will let you know when it is angry.

Whale

Analysis – Large sea mammal which breathes through a blowhole. Whale uses different sound frequencies to communicate. They enjoy family and play.

Interpretation – Seeing a whale is about balancing your emotional bodies and healing of your physical form. It is letting you know that you are clairaudient and can tap into the mind of Great Spirit and bring forth ancient knowledge. This is a time to learn all you need to know and discover your overall destiny.

Wolf

Analysis – A fierce wild animal of the dog family which hunts in packs.

Interpretation – The North American culture believed wolf to be the forerunner of new ideas who returns to the pack to teach and share information and so is recognised as teacher of the tribe. This is the message for you, a time to recognise knowledge that you can share by writing or lecturing to help others better understands their uniqueness or path of life. It is the sharing of great truths that the consciousness of humanity will attain new heights. Also allow yourself to take the time to keep connecting with the teacher within. Do not pretend to be someone other than yourself.

Woodpecker

Analysis – Various and often brightly coloured birds, often depicted as tree tappers. They protect the trees by stopping them becoming infested with insects, excavating holes which become their nesting homes.

Interpretation – Seeing or hearing a woodpecker is about information protecting you from people or situations which take from you. It is a wakeup call to pay attention and get on with life and stop the hurtful irritation.

Worm

Analysis – This creature lives underground slowly eating and regurgitating soil. If it is damaged, it has the ability to continue to live and will re-grow that part of it that has been damaged or died.

Interpretation – Seeing worms is indicating the going over of "what happened" again and again and again. However now it is time to realise that you have created a perfect situation to grow from. The hard work is done. Time to stop hiding away and feeling lowly or humble but instead use your experiences to achieve something new.

Chapter 18

FLOWER SYMBOLISM

Seeing flowers on the mind map can sometimes be recognised as a memory of yours connected to people or places and these memories should be used. Alternatively, the character and symbols of lowers listed here would connect with you.

Alyssum
Interpretation – Spreading pure understanding within a small circle of friends even in emotionally difficult situations and heated encounters.
Anniversary – April

Anemone
Interpretation – Refusal and abandonment. Going away and partings.
Anniversary – Spring and Autumn

Begonia
Interpretation – Gratitude and respect although beware of inconsistency of affections.

Anniversary – Summer

Bluebell
Interpretation – Humility with love, communicating truth and spirituality. Separation and yet everlasting love and closeness to family
Anniversary – April/May

Brambles
Interpretation – This tangled prickly shrub was believed to be the burning bush so bears the flames without being consumed. It is also believed Christ's crown of thorns was made from it. Therefore it represents attempts to destroy but in the end, you achieve by bearing fruit.
Anniversary – Mid April/May

Buttercup
Interpretation – Radiating sunshine and spiritual wisdom everywhere. A free spirit.
Anniversary – April

Carnation
Interpretation – Giver of love. Pink = mother's love, Purple = capriciousness, Red = admiration and deep love, White = pure and ardent love, Yellow = disappointment and rejection.
Anniversary – Early June

Chrysanthemum
Interpretation – Cheerfulness and optimism for a long life of happiness with humility. It can represent an emotional healer.
Anniversary – October

Clover

Interpretation – This is associated with good fortune and luck. Each leaf represents faith, hope, and love and if it is four leaf, also success.

Anniversary – Spring

Cornflower

Interpretation – This represents positive hope for the future and a connection with a clear understanding of nature.

Anniversary – Early Summer

Cowslip

Interpretation – Associated with magic and fairies, they were called fairy cups and used for celebrations.

Anniversary – April/May

Crocus

Interpretation – New beginnings after a long dreary time. A new energy has emerged.

Anniversary – Late March

Daffodil

Interpretation – Rebirth and a new beginning, bringing knowledge and understanding and working with others to bring upliftment.

Anniversary – Late February.

Edelweiss

Interpretation – A star and survivor overcoming cold situation in high places. This flower represents daring and noble courage and being protected.

Anniversary – July.

Forget-me-not
Interpretation – These symbolise true love, faithfulness and respect, and a promise never to forget.
Anniversary – April

Foxglove
Interpretation – These represent being busy and talking a lot. Share their energy with other busy people.
Anniversary – June

Garlic
Interpretation – This strong smelling plant represents a strong presence defending its territory. It stops other plants from being competitors.
Anniversary – April

Heather
Interpretation – Protection from danger and just when you think nothing is there, there is a surprise and your wish comes true. It means good luck for you.
Anniversary – October

Honeysuckle
Interpretation – A complicated affection for a new love or memories of old flames.
Anniversary – June

Hyacinth
Interpretation – A long arduous journey for a short term outcome but this heralds the end of winter, rebirth and healing. It also represents royalty and spirituality.
Anniversary – Early Spring.

Hydrangea
Interpretation – Arrogance and boastfulness but without substance and could easily take over.
Anniversary – Mid Summer.

Iris
Interpretation – A symbol of power, light and hope. The three petals symbolise faith, wisdom and valour. It is dedicated to the Virgin Mary and leads the souls of dead women to heaven.
Anniversary – May

Jasmine
Interpretation – This flower is often used at weddings and other ceremonies and it symbolises sweet but intoxicating love.
Anniversary – June

Lavender
Interpretation – Constancy and loyalty, this flower represents love and steadfast devotion. Is carries health benefits for anxiety, insomnia, depression and restlessness, relaxing the body and healing wounds

Lilac
Interpretation – Acceptance and the first dream of love. Also inspiration.

Lily
Interpretation – Often used as a funeral flower and represents hope of reconciliation.

Marigold
Interpretation – Grief and sorrow. All is not well.

Mushroom
Interpretation – Lives in hiding until the time is right to show itself. There is a hidden agenda which will gain momentum.

Narcissus
Interpretation –The personification of egotism and self conceit. In love with oneself, thus the name narcissist. The scent they give which is painfully sweet is said to cause madness, sending you crazy.

Pansy
Interpretation – Thoughts are with you. Feeling isolated.

Passion Flower
Interpretation – The symbol of passion and a need to be loved and sheltered.

Petunia
Interpretation – Anger and resentment.

Poppy
Interpretation – Eternal sleep, rest and tranquillity for those we have gone before us and who we will always remember.

Primrose
Interpretation – Awakening and the opportunity to make an entrance sharing love.

Rose
Interpretation – White rose is charm, innocence and pure love, Red rose is for deep love, Yellow rose is thoughtful love, Pink rose is caring love or mother love and Deep Pink is for passionate love. However its thorns can hurt.

Snowdrop
Interpretation – The first sign of hope and good things after a period of nothing happening. It can mean overcoming difficulties.

Sunflower
Interpretation – Always reaching for the sunshine and the God light, this flower is about devotion, to stand tall and a refusal to stay down.

Sweet Pea
Interpretation – The need for help to stand tall and to recognise its own beauty.

Tulip
Interpretation – Symbol of a perfect love, charm and beauty. You have moved from a dark place into light and there is an opportunity which if not taken will pass.

Violet
Interpretation – Spiritually grown and confident.

Water Lilly
Interpretation – This flower has grown and made its way from the muddy depths of emotion, reaching for the light of spiritual attainment and the God consciousness. A symbol of mystery and truth.

Wild Flowers
Interpretation – They represent freedom.

Chapter 19

WHERE NEXT

There is more.

Your journey has just begun! Your subconscious is as complex as your present life and therefore this book only represents the beginning of your journey within. What I have not been able to cover within these pages of your frequency patterns and its coded assembly is the interconnection of you with the oneness of all life. I have not been able to cover how to wander through the many time lines stored within its system but truly all the experiences you have ever had can be accessed when you know how.

Now that you have the basic understanding and have experienced your mind map, your exploration begins. You have entered other dimensions of self and can begin to recognise truly who you are, the beginnings of you, and of creation.

It is even possible to find the maps of past lives which are held in the filing system of your experiences beyond your present existence, and these will be found beneath the time sequences on your map. And beyond the beginning of your life in each area there is the connection with your ancestry programming relevant to your present life.

You can even navigate into the future.

How far you travel from the Spiritual Areas of the map is only restricted by the limitations you place on yourself. If you truly wish to know "truth" and not a distorted truth which fits into your present acceptances and indoctrinations, then the wonders of all will unfold.

One to one sittings

One to one private sittings are available with myself and recognised Practitioners. Contact details are listed on the technique website. www.lindabullocktechnique.com

Seminars

Would you like to experience the mind map in a group setting? There are opportunities by attending LBT Seminars. This technique is for anyone to use themselves and with family and friends, and attending seminars will help you to discover so much more than this book can cover. For details of future Seminars contact lbullockenquiries@gmail.com

These seminars will help you to understand how the technique works by giving you the opportunity of experiencing some of the technique for yourself and you will be able to learn from others' experiences. Discover that you are so much more than just the conscious you. Within the subconscious is a store of all your life, past, present and future. Learn how it is possible to communicate with your subconscious through the language it uses and then learn how you can put your life in your hands. These self help levels will teach you how to make the changes you want to make to you and all areas of your life.

Learn how to communicate and analyse:
    1. The state of your emotions.
    2. Your confidence and your strengths and weaknesses.
    3. How balanced a person you are.
    4. How to find the peace you need within you.
    5. You can take a look at your home life, your work life and your social life and decide if you want to change any of them and understand how to do that.
    6. And if you wish, navigate using the technique to discover your future.
    7. Ultimately discover the multi levels of you. So that you can discover who you really are, the real you, rather than accepting and being the person who people and life's circumstances have made feel you are.

Take control and reprogram your life with the Linda Bullock Technique™. Past, present and future are all there for you to access and for you to change if you choose.

Practitioner Training

For those who wish to use the technique professionally there is a training program presently as follows:

> 1. After completing Levels 1&2, practice and experience the technique for yourself.
> 2. Attend a few Level 2 Advanced seminars until you feel confident.
> 3. Then develop case studies with a minimum of 4 healthy client friends or family and a minimum total of 16 x 1 hour session. Keep a record of these sessions and request four of your clients to write a short resume of their experiences and results.
> 4. Book an Evaluation for yourself with Linda or a recognised LBT trainer.
> 5. Then register to attend a Level 3 Assessment Seminar.

On successful completion of level 3, Practitioners will have the use of the Linda Bullock Logo and become a Registered Practitioner of the Linda Bullock Technique™ *with access to insurance cover in the UK and will be listed on the Linda Bullock Technique*™ *website as a recognised Practitioner* (www.lindabullocktechnique.com).

Practitioners are required to pay a licence fee. Included in the licence fee, Practitioners will have contact with Linda or other LBT Trainers with ongoing questions which may arise.

For ongoing training, Practitioners can attend forums to meet with others and discover more knowledge of the creative power of the technique.

Chapter 20

ADDITIONAL NOTES

Your Subconscious will be your guide

Once we have a clear understanding of the map, it is possible to go onto it with a question. The answer will show in the areas relevant and in the time frames relevant as your subconscious directs you to them.

As well as working with addictions to things like cigarettes and sugar I have also been experimenting with people who have physical health problems with some good results and these experiments continue.

With myself, I had noticed that my lifetime of having cold feet had in my later years extended right up my legs. So my legs were freezing cold and I was beginning to have difficulty walking with ease. One of our Practitioners, who noticed my difficulty climbing stairs and suggested I look on the map to find the problem.

I was directed by my subconscious to the very back of the wood and there, connected to my wood was my mother's wood from her map. My mother had had difficulty with rheumatics in her legs throughout the latter part of her life and eventually could not stand and needed to be hoisted to move. But connected also to her map and my map was her father's wood and his father's wood and on close examination of their woods, I realised that there was a hereditary link between us all, with each of us suffering with the same leg circulation problems. I disconnected their maps from mine and then asked my subconscious if I needed to go anywhere else on my map and dealt with some other experiences relevant to my cold legs and the results were immediate. My legs and feet are now warm.

Of course there are people with major health problems and I am in the process of discovering where and how the technique can help them. I always say to the clients in my experimenting that there are no guarantees.

Missing Crucial Information

When following the mind map by yourself it is easy to miss important information. An example would be that when looking at the wood/forest/trees, they may be tangled together and because you enjoy walking in the woods in your material world, you believe that all of them look like that and it is normal. After all where have you seen on earth a perfectly formed wood with the trees all perfectly spaced and light showing through in all areas?

But what needs to be recognised always when on the mind map, is that this is the language of the subconscious, and you need to look at the picture in a completely different way.

When a wood is tangled, each tree is in the process of being suffocated as there is not sufficient air for the tree to breath, and it will eventually die, so remembering that each tree is an aspect of you, that aspect of you will eventually be destroyed and stop existing.

But there is an added piece of information in this picture. If you think that what you are looking at is normal, you will also believe that, in your life, there is not possibility of situations being any different. The picture is telling you that you are putting up with the way your life is.

Remember that when you are close to the picture of each area, you might also be experiencing the feeling relevant to what you are looking at. In the example just sited, the feeling is that you cannot change anything because that is the way it is. You can realise from examples like this that you need support by being helped by someone else like one of the LBT Practitioners or alternatively, come right off the map, and then re enter making sure you "step back" or "elevate slightly" when you near the area, so that you can then look at the situation from a distance sufficient to detach from that obstacle and then get your subconscious or kingdom helpers to make the relevant changes.

May be on the ground in an area of the mind map, there is moss and you think to yourself that you like it because it is soft to walk on. Yes, there is a message here that from a bad experience you have managed to make the best of it, but you have moved away from the full understanding of the picture and it is necessary to research the symbol of what you are seeing.

Moss grows in waterlogged ground where nothing else can grow. Water is emotion, so where did that water come? Usually it is from heavy rain storms which represent situations in your life where the emotion, not from you, but from others and other situations, has destroyed any possibility of you creating new experiences because nothing can grow.

Alternatively, on examining the source of the water, you discover that there is an underground stream. It will in that scenario be necessary to investigate the streams origin. Xray vision can be used for this. Maybe you will find the spring which started that stream journey, or maybe there

is a connection from "the" stream, which flooded over and destroyed trees, and then that emotion was buried and eventually made the land waterlogged. Or maybe the water came from "the" lake.

There are so many examples which you can become aware of, each explaining the journey you experienced which has brought you to this point where moss is growing. Just removing the moss will not solve the problem. The source of the water needs to be removed, whether it is clouds and rain or a stream or underground lake or whatever other picture you see. And then the water in the ground needs to be removed together with the moss and arrangements made for fertile soil to replace it and those changes will completely change the dynamics of your life.

Remember not to bury pictures because they will then still exist. And it is no good putting another picture over the first picture you saw. This would cause complications in your life. For example you cannot plant trees on top of other trees or create a new lake on top of the old one. Can you imagine what you are actually creating for yourself if you did this?

Your Material World Changes

I know I am repeating myself, but it is really important not to remove things from your material areas of your mind map.

While removal of obstacles, whatever they are, from the three inner areas of the wood, stream and lake, is merely removing those things which are affecting you in a negative way, when you are dealing with the material world areas of the harbour, beach, building, garden and village/town/city you have to realise the possible non intentional changed it can make to your world.

An example might be that you have to work with someone who makes your life miserable and when you find your work building in the village you decide to find them and remove them. Now this is important to take notice of. What will happen if you do that is that you will no longer be working with them. However, that might not mean that they lose their job or move to another employer. What it might mean is that you lose your job and have to move to another employer. So not a good idea.

Be careful not to get angry with your partner and think it will be a good idea to remove them from the building (your home life). The consequences will be that you will no longer be together and it may be permanent but how this comes about is out of your hands.

So improve and don't remove in your material areas unless you know exactly what you are doing and what the result of that will be.

Connecting with the Spirit World

For those who have attended seminars, you will know that there are the areas on the mind map where you can meet and talk with your departed loves ones and for those who work with the Spirit World either as a healer or medium, there is also on the mind map, an area where you can meet with your Spirit guides so you can find the answers to any questions you have.

But there is more. We all have a Spiritual Advisor who you can meet to ask for advice about your spiritual journey through life.

Connecting with your subconscious which is the conduit of all of your experiences and therefore the programming of your life is only part of the understanding of who you really are. You are a multifaceted being who may for most of your life have believed that the only truth is that you only exist in a conscious three dimensional life.

You may have heard the saying that all the answers are within, and by using the LBT mind map, you can access all knowledge and understanding of the many dimensions of you which exist right now. And you can discover all you wish to know about this planet and the universe. You can also connect with your Spirit and discover your life purpose and so much more.

There is a Whole Universe Within and That Universe Has It's Own Language.

Changes to the subconscious map have to be changed with the language of your subconscious, by symbols. So it is not uncommon to see workmen and machinery doing those changes. For instance, if the changes need road workers, that is what will show up in the picture. If it is gardeners or landscape designers who are needed, likewise they will come to do the work. So don't be surprised if these workmen are what you see. They are only the representation of the symbolic intelligence of your subconscious.

Your subconscious uses its own language. I often say that your subconscious is like Google. On that level of consciousness there is a "oneness". So not surprising that whatever is needed can be accessed. It might be that you need a bank manager or a financial advisor. These are not actual "people" but are the connections of the intelligence within you to all knowledge.

If you, in this world, do not trust anyone because of your life experience then your subconscious knows that, and will not show you "people" but will find some way to accommodate your needs. Perhaps it will be "little people", "fairies or angels or animals". If that is what you would trust then your subconscious will bring them into the picture.

If you are determined while on your mind map to change everything yourself, it is because in this life you are living, you believe that everything has to be done by you. Again, experience may have taught you that "if a job is to be done well, you might as well do it yourself" or perhaps people have let you down.

There is no need for you to do these changes to your subconscious yourself because it only means that you are too close to the picture. Stand back or elevate from it and allow your subconscious to deal with how the changes should be made.

Your Magic Kingdom

I often describe the subconscious world as a magic kingdom when I am working with children. And I like to think of it in that way myself.

You are the "ruler", the prince, or princess or king or queen. Using this analogy helps us to understand the system. The conscious us has to give the instructions and then the subconscious us follows those instructions. Royalty are not going to do plumbing or building work. They employ someone to do it. Likewise, you only need to give clear instructions and the work will be done.

Instructions may be "Make that building a perfect building where I have all I need to be happy" or "Create an easy to walk, happy path" or "Remove all dirty water" or "Change the levels of the ground" or "Remove that mountain" or "Heal that tree and give it all the nutrients, space and light it needs to be alive". Nothing is impossible for your subconscious.

A Different Language

When you enter your mind map of your subconscious, your thoughts are your communication and navigation. However, your subconscious knows what your real "intention" is and this is not always the words you formulate.

It might be that you ask to see the truth of a difficult decision you have to make in life but really you don't want to look at it. So the subconscious is receiving two opposing messages at the same time and can only give you half of the answer.

Or you look at the picture presented to you and cannot see anything wrong with it. An example might be, your trees are in the dark or the roots of the trees are not in the ground. If you see this picture as normal, it will probably be that you don't expect anything else for yourself and have come to accept your lot.

Another example relevant to the building (home life), was where someone who, when they went home had no peace. Their family wanted their attention all of the time. When looking on the map at the building they were also aware of a garden at the back of the building.

If you are looking at and aware of the building and see a garden, it will not be THE garden. Unless you are high up looking at your map and are not on ground level or just above ground level, you can only see the area you are in. THE garden is a completely separate area.

On this occasion, the garden at the back of the house was completely dead, meaning no peace at home. The subconscious was instructed to make the garden a beautiful alive place where this person would love to spend time. However, the subconscious only created a garden area half the size than was first seen.

When this person went home, instead of her family meeting her with what they needed from her, the family were nowhere to be seen. She presumed they had gone out but then realised that they were in a different part of the house. This lady spend two and half hours undisturbed – and then the family came to pester her.
She then realised that, although she "instructed" changing the subconscious map, there was another part of her which would not want her family not to be there and "need her". Her subconscious has received both messages and following both instructions, only gave her part of her "verbal instruction".

Connecting with Different Time Frames

Anyone who wishes to go into their subconscious mind map with a question needs to understand its language and the many levels of time before they can.

The map is like a filing system of every moment of your life and even connects with ancestry and past lives, so anyone trying to go in with a question, who has not become acquainted with its complexities, can get completely lost.

When we first go into the three "inner areas", the wood, the stream and the lake, we first see "present time" or how things are right now. When we choose to, we can trace back in time but will find the "past only relevant to the present".

In the material world areas, we see "present time" and if the picture we see is changing or we make changes, we will be seeing the future. But there are other pictures, from the past, in the filing system.

Removing things from the Map

The benefit of this technique is that when you remove obstacles and restrictions from the picture, you will be removing these from your life and they will no longer exist in the program filing system. And it is necessary to remove these symbolic obstacles with symbols. Putting a picture on top of the picture seen will only work like "positive thinking" and will manifest for a while but the problem will still exist to rise up another day. So you should use symbols to remove symbols.

Example – Removing dirty water from the inner three areas of the map, forest, stream and lake area, has to be seen to be happening by you and so something like drain suckers or some suction pipe would be necessary to do this to take the dirty water completely away from the map so out of the picture and out of your subconscious.

Another example would be, if a large rock is an obstacle to your going forward or is preventing you from seeing ahead clearly. In this case something like a digger or crane might be useful. If you are a person who normally does everything in life yourself, you may find that you need to instruct your subconscious clearly how the process is to happen but ultimately, once you realise it, the intelligence of the subconscious will know exactly what to use and how to use it and where to remove it to.

Creating a perfect forest, stream or lake picture in your mind and putting it on the picture in front of you only works like positive thinking and those obstacles will continue to affect you. To explain what I mean as an analogy, imagine a glass with particles of muddy soil in it. If you put fresh soil on top of that muddy soil, the muddy soil will still exist in the glass. However, if you remove the muddy soil first and then fill the glass with fresh soil, that fresh soil will not be affected and spoiled. I hope that analogy helps as you change your subconscious programming.

Hard to Remove

If, after instructing the removal of any obstacles or anything, which you no longer wish to be a part of your programming, there seems to be a difficulty to remove it then your subconscious is informing you to take a closer look and ask the question "what is the problem" or "why is it taking so long" and then once that question is asked you will be given the answer.

Your subconscious is an intelligent part of you but cannot control your life and has to take instruction from you. It is one of the laws of the universe that you have free will and unless and until you inform your subconscious what is acceptable to you, it has to follow previous instructions.

An example of a previous instruction – If you have been told and programmed by life's experiences that you will never succeed or you have to suffer in this life, that will be held in your subconscious as an instruction from you until you change it.

Remember the Perfect Picture

The forest should be full of healthy, happy, alive trees as far as you can see in the forest area, all with the nutrients in the soil which they need and all spaced to let light everywhere in the forest so the trees can all grow to their full potential.   There should be no restrictions on the ground preventing you from walking into the forest in any direction. The sky should be clear and blue.

The stream should be crystal clear water running from right to left with no restrictions and no obstacles in it for its whole length from start to present time and the water should be sitting in the bed of the stream. Not too little or too much water. The sky should be clear and blue

The lake should be still and be crystal clear water so you can see to the bottom of the lake at the deepest point without anything on the lake or in the lake or at the bottom of the lake or buried under the bottom of the lake, causing disturbance. The sky should be clear and blue.

The Wisdom tree should be healthy, happy, alive and in perfect soil giving it the nutrients it needs so it can grow to its full potential.

Anything in the above pictures which prevent them from being perfect pictures needs to be understood and changed or removed.

Pay Attention to Your Subconscious

While you subconscious cannot make decisions about your life, it will support and help you to achieve whatever you wish. Because it is recording in its language every moment of your life, it already knows your intention when you enter the map and will guide you to know the information you need.

Everything on the map is information and your subconscious will give "hints" to help you find the right answers so try not to ignore anything you see. There is no information "fill ins". Every small detail is relevant.

"All The Answers Are Within"

They really are and if you can think of a question you can find the answer whether that is about you and your emotions and balance etc. or your material world, or your Spiritual connections.

One of the areas on the mind map I would like to remind you about is the <u>field leading to the hill</u>. The journey to the side of the hill is often by using a hot air balloon but you can also fly or jump to it. Even the way you journey there is information and if it is in a hot air balloon, the colour of the balloon is also information regarding your reason for taking the journey or the question you have set.

Why do we take that journey and what is there?

On the side of the hill you have a few choices of who you meet from the Spirit World.

It may be an expert who you have requested to help you see your life – Together you can look down on the map and see your life from a Spiritual "point of view". Going with an question will allow your subconscious to give you the advice you need and from there it is possible to go down to the various areas of your map to see clearly the problem and be advised how to deal with it or them. Always return to the side of the hill and then come back the same way you travelled, back to the field, onto the path and back to the beginning where you started your journey.

Also on the side of the hill you can meet with your Spiritual Guides. For those who work with the Spirit World in any way, including with mediumship or healing, you can request that particular guides are there to meet and talk to you.

Always begin the conversation. The Spirit World have to abide by the law of the universe which is "your free will" and cannot tell you what to do but can give you advice. It is up to you to ask for that advice and to keep the conversation going.

The communication on the side of the hill can be telepathy which is thought transference, or it might be clairaudience so that you hear the words, usually in your mind, depending how you normally communicate with the Spirit World.

You may wish to meet on the side of the hill with a relative or friend who is in Spirit. It is there where we can meet again and know that we have not lost them except their physical presence. Perhaps it is an opportunity to mend bridges with someone you had a disagreement with in life or had difficulty getting on with. What could not be sorted in this world can be sorted there.

Or you may, like me, wish to offer an open invitation that whoever would like to come and speak to you from the spirit world would be welcome.

It is even possible to speak to the spirit of someone who is still alive and discuss any situation between you and them.

Also on the side of the hill is your Spiritual Advisor who you will find in a cave. If you intend to go to the cave make sure you have a question before you even go onto the map. In that way, you can be shown the answer symbolically as soon as you enter the cave and then communicate – you start the conversation asking to understand what you are being shown – to have the answer confirmed.

The top of the hill is your connection with the planet and the universe. Again if you intend to visit the top of the hill prepare a question you wish to know about the earth or the universe and then someone will be waiting for you when you get there. Usually connected to the answer at the top of the hill you will be aware of visual pictures.

The questions you have on any area of the hill would be actioned by "a need to know" within you. There is always a question on that level as well as on a verbal level.

And then there is the <u>meadow area</u>. I remind you that here you have the opportunity to meet with your light, your higher self, your spirit – whatever you would like to call that part of your which dwells in the dimension of light and yet is connected to you at all times. Do you remember who you were before the world told you who you are. Well you can discover that here because it is about being aware of you and it is your opportunity to connect and eventually stay connected in your perception.

Once connected with that light you can then connect with your <u>group soul</u> and beyond that, the <u>universal mind</u> and its many aspects, which we have come to call God. "From the source we came and to the source we return" – not in some far distant time and space but right here using the mind map to find your way.

All of the experiences you have in the field/hill and meadow areas need to be evidence to you and that will often come because of the feeling or emotion connected with the experiences you have.

How Areas Interconnect

The Mind Map into our subconscious takes the form it does for many reasons. It is correct that we could take each area "off the map" and use those areas individually but it does not allow the interconnections of the areas to give a bigger picture and therefore it creates restrictions of information.

The wood, stream and lake areas are positioned to allow the picture to give us the added information of how, sometimes, the stream may overflow into the wood or travel to the lake, or even something like the lake draining underground to the building or the village/town etc.

It has been suggested that the areas can be rearranged but I do not believe that could ever work. Its creation is unique and while it takes a simple form, we must also recognise that it is complex.

As we enter each area on the ground level, everything we see is relevant to that area. For instance, if we see a stream in the wood, it is relevant to the wood and may have come from a spring in the wood and not THE stream. If we elevated just above the trees and see a lake behind the trees, it is not THE lake but A lake, created maybe from rain water, and is relevant to the wood. We do not see THE stream or THE lake until we actually go to those areas or, if we elevate high above the map, it is possible to look down and see all of the individual areas below us. In other words the whole map.

The wood, stream and lake are in the order they are because, it is important that we first look at our wood and make changes to build our confidence by making sure that all the trees are strong and healthy and have enough room, light and all the nutrients they need, so they can grow to their full potential, before we go to the stream to look at our emotions. Only after we have made changes to these two areas, will we be ready to look at the Lake area which represents how balanced we are and of course can show depression. So there is perfect order to the map.

Looking at the Whole Picture

When I started working with the inner areas on the map, the wood, the stream and the lake, many years ago, I believed that I had to meticulously work with each symbol in an area as I came across them, but later I realised that, while each symbol was important to understand, the overall picture must also be seen and understood.

As an example, when we travel along the stream in the direction the water is flowing to us, we see emotional memories of the past, of things like waterfalls which represent going emotionally over the edge, lakes representing a time of emotional imbalance, underground streams when we buried our emotions and many other obstacles along the way. But if we change each aspect/symbol individually, it takes a long time and effort.

So travelling the whole length of the stream and getting the picture and story of the whole length before making changes, allows us to alter the whole picture in one go. This creates instant results for the person.

The Village/Town/City

The village, town or even city represents the working and social parts of our lives and may be in two separate areas showing the working life and social life as very separate if in fact that is true of our material lives. Each building is our building – something we connect with, something we do.

When we first see the village/town, the buildings we see will always be relevant to our lives right now – present time. So if we are visiting a doctor or hospital in our lives, we will see the symbolic buildings representative of those connections. Otherwise they will not show in the immediate picture.

If we visit a relative regularly, there will be the symbolic building for where they live and we visit. If we work, there will be a symbol representing our work. If we have a spiritual belief and meet up with others, there will probably be a church symbolising that. To understand what each building represents, we only need to question with our minds and the answer comes immediately.

Investigating each building outside and inside gives a great insight into life relevant to it at the time.

Health Possibilities

Sometimes, from my experiences, just making the alterations and improvements to the wood, stream and lake can have significant results on our health.

A recent example was a client whose stream originated in a sea/ocean. Of course, if the stream originated from there it would be salt water, and this middle aged client had been ill for the whole of her life. I think we can all agree that many health issues can originate from our emotions. Just altering the client's stream gave instant improvements to her health.

Another example which I have encountered is many people, who in their past, have buried, held back or shut down their stream and therefore their own emotions. Then tracing along the stream discovered, in more recent times, a new stream which has been created from rain water or from a melted glacier. This is not their emotions. It is emotions taken from someone else or some situation.

As long as they carry within their subconscious those past hidden emotional experiences, this continues to impact on their lives and particularly their health.

With people with these experiences it is necessary to find out where their own emotion stream has stopped and where that water has gone. This is all part of finding the whole story and being able to correct the map into a perfect crystal clear stream which is only their own emotions.

Removing rain water, icy water if created from rain or snow, and salt water, if there has been a connection with the ocean, is vital to help the person regain emotional happiness. And in the process, it is amazing how many health problems are also sorted.

Not to be Played With

There are many examples of people "playing" with this and not realising the power of it.

The subconscious is the power behind our life, controlling and running your experiences. Like a computer, once the program is installed, it will give the answers only from what is a part of that program.

So believing that you are a failure or hopeless in some area, will continue and perpetuate from the past experiences which became stored in the information of your subconscious. Something like, a parent or school teacher or boss who says something negative to you. As long as that imprint is stored in your subconscious, it will be your programming and you will draw to you similar experiences, either from other people or from life.

This is why, in the inner areas, it is necessary to "see" any obstacles or restrictions shown as symbols, "removed". If you only "change the picture", it has the same effect like burying the problem and it will still be there in your subconscious programming and you will have put a picture on a picture.

If you try to remove, say a wall, from any of the inner areas, but it does not move immediately, or does not move at all, very often it is your subconscious drawing your attention to other connections to it.

An example, a wall in front of the wood, does not move when you give the instruction. When you question "why?" you become aware that under the ground it is set in concrete. So you instruct to also have that concrete removed. But still, nothing is taken away. So a closer look again, shows that the concrete has been pored over roots of trees which are holding the concrete down.

What we have here a story of why that wall was built. Knowing who the roots of the trees belonged to can give an answer. In this case it was the ancestry tree roots. So a family indoctrination was the cause. Until we have the whole picture, nothing moves. But then, the instruction can be to remove the wall, the concrete and the tree roots. If you have the whole story, they will all now be easily and quickly removed.

Your subconscious is a living intelligence and it is "yours", a part of you. However, the conscious you is in charge of your life, the boss, and your "subconscious you" cannot change your life for you but it will help you once it is asked.

Another example, a client is taken to the lake area but when invited to look at the wisdom tree, is unable to turn to look. They realised that their attention is drawn to another tree in the distance. Here the subconscious is helping them to recognise, by not letting them turn, that their wisdom is no longer the tree on their left, but the tree "in the wrong place".

On closer inspection, the tree which is set to their left, is dead and needs to be removed and replaced with the tree they are looking at.

A point to make here is that everything on the map should be exactly in the "right" place according to the map and if anything is out of place, it is information to be questioned.

The reason for the change of tree was relevant to the client's life experiences but also to changes they had made on the mind map. So their way of thinking was now dead and not beneficial any more. Your wisdom tree is your wisdom from your life experiences and new life experiences can change that tree.

Remember that as you enter the map, everything you see is "present time". Other time frames can be navigated but only time frames relevant to the now will be found. That includes past and future. Even the future can change when we alter the present.

There have been experiments with the technique and for some people, it is a stepping stone into other understandings. For example, the discovery through our journeying on the map, that we are multifaceted and connected on those other levels of us, to a oneness. This is for you to experience rather than me telling you so. And you will only discover it if you want to open your mind to truth.

Working With a Practitioner

The Linda Bullock Technique™ is a MIND map and therefore it is more complex to follow than an ordinary map. There are many time levels and while just doing onto the map without a purpose will give you "present time" information, each area is capable of moving in time. So if you go onto the map with a question, each area will change to show you the answer if it is relevant to past experiences. For example, if your home life, when you were young, is part of the answer, you will see the symbol relevant to that time.

When you are on the map you are connected to the intelligence of your subconscious which will support you on your journey. Questions you ask with your mind will be answered in the language of the subconscious, but if you don't ask the question, the information you see can seem difficult to understand. Interaction with the subconscious is an important part of the communication and understanding of the technique.

When sitting as a client with a Practitioner, you will realise the important of the Practitioner explaining the symbolic meanings and prompting you to ask what something you are seeing represents. The Practitioner is a guide supporting you on your journey and there to explain that that everything is information. But you are in charge.

When you are working by yourself on the map, it is easy to miss symbols and information and particularly not recognise and be aware of how you are feeling while on the map. An example might be that you do not know that the symbol is a problem because in life you do not realise this and are used to it. There is also the feeling you may have, that there is nothing you can do about what you are looking at, or you may not know how to change it. Again this feeling represents your normal way of looking at this problem in life.

Nothing is shown to you that does not represent information. Nothing is there on the map just to fill in as an extra part of the picture. Not seeing the picture clearly is not a visualising problem you have, but instead is information about something preventing you from seeing clearly.

More Details about The Lake Surroundings

The surrounding area of the lake is relevant to what is affecting your balance at the moment.

When you first look at the Lake area, you are looking at the symbols which represent present time situations which are affected the balance and harmony within you. This could be positive or negative information.

As an example, we may see mountains surrounding the lake or one mountain. Mountains can be about achievement – we climb mountains to get to the top – so they would normally represent some situation in your life which you wish to succeed at. Are you climbing those mountains at the moment? Alternatively and depending on the picture you see, the mountains could be obstacles in your way.

Being aware of more details about the mountains might be important. For instance, details about whether the mountains would cast a shadow on the lake and therefore make the lake less easy to see. This might cause you to be less able to see how balanced you are

Easy to climb mountains mean exactly that, that you will climb them easily, and therefore this could be a positive which helps you feel balanced in life. But if the mountains are difficult to climb, that would be a negative. Maybe they are ice capped, which would be telling you that the climb could be treacherous and that you would feel isolated and in the cold if and when you reach the top. Or are you there already.

Perhaps they are grey and rocky, the grey meaning depressing and not giving you any colour in your life, and rocky meaning they are hard and difficult to climb. Or are they covered in grass which might seem a good symbol of new ways upwards and being able to have a great view of everything from that perspective (think of the movie The Sound of Music). Or are there trees on the side of it, meaning that you are putting a lot of your effort and capabilities, into climbing that mountain. Remember that trees anywhere on the map are you.

If the mountains are in the distance they could be mountains you know you are going to climb, but not yet, or are those opportunities out of reach? Be aware that the information is in the detail.

Maybe there is a building or a house by the lake. It would be telling you that your home life or work or social connections are affecting you. Investigating the building will give you the symbolic understanding of that connection.

The sky should be blue if you are not being affected by outside problem influences or situations. Clouds would create shadow over the picture which makes it more difficult to see. Storm clouds are even more negative a situation from outside of your world and map, and would indicate that there are arguments or aggression from other people or situations which are already creating problems for you, particularly, in this area. If the clouds begin to make rain, your lake would be affected and disturbed on the surface, and therefore your balance and harmony would be affected by that.

Is the sun shining on the picture? The sun gives us warmth and light but is it preventing you from seeing the lake properly. Question in your thoughts what that means and you will instantly know the answer.

Grass surrounding the lake gives the impression of freedom and happy times if the grass is cut and fresh. But maybe the grass is long and neglected and there may be problems like rocks which you could fall over or holes you might fall into because you cannot see them. Or even a snake in the grass which might represent an untrustworthy or deceitful person. If the grass is long you may be unaware of any difficulties or danger you are in.

Analysis and Then Transformation

Remember that whatever is seen is to be analysed first. When someone says that they do not have the ability to visualise, that is not correct. The analysis of this is showing that the area they are in is showing that, they cannot see it clearly in their life.

For example, if the path cannot be seen, the person cannot see where to go in life. So, "no path for them in life" and "no way forward in life".

Likewise, any area not seen clearly, or not at all, means that the subconscious is giving them the information and it is not a problem with the persons capabilities.

Elevating or stepping back will allow the picture to be seen more clearly. Usually from there, what can then be seen, is something like a black hole or a tunnel or mist, fog, low lying cloud, or something which is preventing the picture from being seen. Each of these symbols can then be analysed and understood and then a decision can be made how to deal with removing that symbol and that problem.

Always look at the path before standing on it. Otherwise you have already stepped into the future. And also, it is not wise to step onto the path without knowing how it is. For example, you may be stepping into a black hole or onto something like broken glass, and this will only make you feel the situation even stronger.

Time frames are important to understand. The path immediately in front of you is present time but as you look further along the path from where you are standing, at the beginning, you will be looking into the future path of life situation. Someone standing at the beginning of the path, who only knows where they are going in say, the next week or month, will only be able to see a short path. Whereas someone who knows exactly where they are going in life in the future will see a much longer path ahead of them.

Likewise all the areas on the map show present time when you first get to that area. It is only when you begin to look beyond the frontage of trees or in the stream area, along where the stream is flowing from or in the lake area, beneath the lake that you will be looking at the past.

The above is only if you have just "visited each area" to have a look at your life and you have not gone in with a specific question. Posing a question will mean that your subconscious may answer that question in the relevant areas with different times in your life for each of the areas. So you will be shown different time frames.

In the material areas, again the first picture seen will be present time but when the picture is changing in front of you, you will be seeing the future unfolding. Also when the picture is changed by yourself, you are creating the future relevant to that area.

I remind you that changes in the three inner areas are instant but changes in the material world areas will take whatever time is needed to bring the result about.

The Sea

We all understand the sea to be the outside world. Normally we look at the sea/ocean when we are at the harbour and it is relevant to what we are trying to achieve in life, and we also notice the sea when we are at the beach. However, the sea can show up in any of the areas but only if it is relevant.

The Wood area – sometimes the sea/ocean is seen at the back of the wood. As the wood should be trees everywhere, it tells us that in the past, the world drowned and therefore destroyed that person. To correct this, we would need to have the sea/ocean tide used to take it back and out of sight. Then the ground where it was would probably have to be removed as there is probably salt in it and no good planting trees only for them to not survive. The next step would be to replace the ground with good fertile soil and replant trees there.

The Stream Area – Whenever and wherever the sea/ocean is seen along the stream, it represents being lost emotionally. Think of it this way, if a fresh water stream flows into the sea/ocean, you will not be able to find it in the salt water. If the stream flows from the sea/ocean, it will be salt water and, very often, the person will suffer with their health and will find it difficult to succeed at anything they try to do. You will know from the seminars how to counteract this.

The Lake Area – If the sea/ocean flows into the lake or the lake is open to the sea/ocean, there will be a connection where the outside world has caused the person to be "out of balance" or depressed by what the outside world has done to them.

The Building – Some people have said that when they see the sea/ocean from the building that they believe they will live near it. However, we have to remind ourselves that everything is symbolic and therefore it would mean that their home life would have some connection with the outside world.

The Village/Town/City – Remembering that this area is the social and working areas of your life then there will again be some connection to the outside world.

The Path – It would mean that your path of life will take you to the outside world.

Getting Too Close to the Picture

Going on the map by your self is not always easy. There is more information than just the pictures you see. Stored in your subconscious is also "feelings" connected to those pictures.

An example might be that as you approach the stream you see that it is either running very quickly or overflowing and you begin to get emotional. At this point you are connecting with the emotion as well as seeing the problem. Being able to take a step back from the stream or elevating will stop that emotion but it is not always easy to do when you are on the map by yourself. Working with someone else who knows the map is of great help because they can be aware that you are experiencing that emotion and help you either step back or elevate.

Another example might be that when you visit your wood you fall asleep. I was told by someone who was using the CD I produced that she never got past the wood and it must have been the background music which caused her to fall asleep. When you are on the map you are in a slight altered state of consciousness and everything you experience is information. She had just got too close to the trees which were very tired, just as she was in life. Her working life was just too busy at that time.

A Different View

If you are facing difficulties in your life or wish to trace back in time to difficulties in your life and are going onto the map by yourself, this can be done from the hillside from where you can look down onto your life map. Ask for an expert to be waiting there on the hill to help you. Of course, from the hill, you will be looking at your map from a spiritual perspective. And from the hill you can fly down to any area and then fly back to the hill. Whenever you go on the map always return the same way that you went. So if you have travelled to the hill and then visited other areas of the map always return to the hill and come back from there.

Who Do You Trust?

If you are the sort of person who feels that if a job is to be done properly then you have to do it yourself, or if life has taught you that you cannot trust others to help you, or if you are alone in life with no help, then probably you will want to do any work on the map yourself. Alternatively if you ask the subconscious for changes to be made and you see workers coming in to the do that work, you are accepting that help is available.

What I find interesting is that, when we see workers, they will be perfect for the job in hand. What we are looking at are symbols of these experts. So, if the work is on the path, we often see road workers. If the work is to be done in the garden, gardeners will show up. If we are in the health area, we may see doctors or surgeons. In the wood, tree experts. All of them are still the intelligence of your subconscious shown in symbolic form.

Occasionally, animals come to do the work and they will be giving us information. An example is of a mole when I was working with a client. I realised that there would be a lot of underground work. So the subconscious was bringing the attention to look underground. Looking up the character or symbol of an animal you see will give you more information about the situation.

The Building and the Position of the Garden

I have noticed that some people get a bit confuses with these two areas and for clarification, when you are at the building area, you may see a garden. This garden may be at the front, side or even back of the building but is still relevant to the building and your home life. Even still the garden represents "peace" so can be used as relevant to your home.

At the front of the building it would probably represent that just thinking about your home gives you a sense of peace, or as you approach your home you feel at peace. At the side or back of the building, it probably means that although home is not always peaceful, you can sometimes escape within in it and find a space which is peaceful.

Therefore, if you are still aware of the building when you see the garden, you are not actually in the separate area of "the" garden. Remember that "the" garden has to be completely separate with no awareness of the building.

Why Subconscious and Not Unconscious

I have heard that Professionals in talking therapies etc call it the unconscious but my experience through this technique has found it to be alive and aware and intelligent so I will continue to call it the "Subconscious" for want of a better word.

What you discover through this mind map is what an incredible multifaceted human you are.

The Path

If you intend looking at the path rather than just stepping onto A path, "look before you leap". The point is that some people have terrible paths like "a black hole" or "broken glass" or "a dark tunnel" or a "swamp" and by stepping onto it, they may actually be engulfed by it.

Although I have in the past always started the journey onto the map by looking first at the path, now I often use "the path" as "a path" – not looking at it and therefore making it an access way. The problem can be that if there is a lot of work to do there, this can take up a lot of unnecessary time. Instead if we make changes to the inner areas, the wood, the stream and the lake, the path will automatically change by itself. After making these changes to the inner areas return to the beginning of the path, turn and look at it then. If the changes to the inner worlds have been made properly, the path will have changed to a perfect path.

When looking at the path, immediately in front of you will be present time, and if you can see further ahead you will know where you are going in the future. People who only see a short part of the path will not be sure of where they are going in the future.

Each area of the map is an individual area when you access it on ground level or just slightly elevated above and therefore anything seen on either side of the path is only relevant to the path. If you turn left onto the wood area, the same picture on the left of the path will not be seen. It is only when we go high above the map that we can see all the areas, and if, and how, they interconnect.

The Sky

A clear blue sky is always the optimum as it represents the outside world and indicates that you have a clear view of it. Storm clouds are emotions from other people or situations which are affecting you emotionally (the rain) and putting you or the area in the dark. White clouds still cast a shadow making it more difficult to see aspects of you and your life. It is possible to question who or what is making the clouds to have a clear understanding and to see who or what is in them and therefore in the picture. Whether clouds can be moved from the ground depends of their thickness and if they come from another area of your map or even across the sea from someone else's map. The work then has to be done from a higher view point.

If you see the sun or the moon or stars, these are symbols which can be interpreted. Night time is a time of rest before a new day and a new beginning but it may be a time of feeling in the dark and not realising what is next in your life.

The sky is not always the same over each of the areas and therefore when visiting each area, being aware of the sky is part of the picture.

How Much Detail

How we approach the information on the map tells us a lot about ourselves. Someone who in the normal life has to give their attention to detail like an architect etc, will notice more details on the map whereas someone who always sees the overall picture will be less aware of the small stuff. When working with clients I am aware of both the details and the overall picture. I often have an extra awareness of the story and can prompt a client to look closer if I "feel" it is important. I am always looking for being able to achieve the most in the time available. That tells you a lot about me.

Each Practitioner will have their own way of approaching the information. Some will take more time and care and others will be quick to cover ground. That will always show who and how they are.

The Subconscious Knows

Really it does. It knows your capabilities to understand the pictures and where you will find the answer to a symbol or the character of that symbol. The altered state of consciousness which you enter when entering the map is not time restricted or knowledge restricted.

Areas Within Areas

Although on a normal map, where you see drawn a lake and tree and island itemised, then when you actually visit that place, you would expect to see all three at the same time, but the technique map is very different. We navigate the technique with our intention and so this must be taken into consideration.

In the lake area, we would normally first look at the wisdom tree and that represents one area. Very often the lake will not be seen at the same time as you see the tree, unless it is relevant to wisdom. Then, when the intention is to look at the lake, that is another separate are, and usually you will not see the island until you decide to look for it. So there are three separate areas to this part of the map.

I hope you can follow me with this information –
If you see the lake when you are looking at the tree, the lake is "relevant" to your wisdom.
If, when you intend to look at the lake you see the island, you are in the lake area and health is relevant to your balance situation at the moment.
Once you reach the island, if you are aware of the lake, the lake needs to be used relevant to your health.

Likewise there are two areas of the harbour part of the map. When you first approach the harbour, the sea or ocean will not normally be seen. It is not until you decide to look out towards the sea, that you will see it.

And there is also the building area. If you are aware of a garden at the same time as you view the building, whether it is in front of , at the side of or behind the building, it is relevant to the building area. It is not until you move away from the building to find the garden, that you will reach the garden (peace) area.

Flowers

Flowers have a universal symbolism and these can easily be checked on Search Engines on the Internet. That symbol is being represented in whichever area of the map they are found. But they may also be a memory to you. An example might be potted Hyacinths which your mother grew. And then add to that the meaning of the flower representing a long arduous journey to overcome and hiding in the dark until you could show yourself. They also represent skin irritations so the story here might be that this persons mother caused them to be in the dark (could not see clearly) until they could come into their own and the emotion from that experience may have created a skin condition.

Flowers also represent times of the year when they bloom and this could be an anniversary of someone you know or of you, so quite a lot of information can be gained from that flower you saw.

And remember to use the colour of the flower.

The Language of Symbolism

The whole world and universe is the language of symbolism. Anyone who has looked into numerology will understand that all letters and number have a sound resonance which equates to symbolism. It is as if we are living in an amazing computerised reality where the mind within all atoms is connected to every other atom and its energy.

We are, all the time, being programmed within this world intelligence. The names we are given and the dates we are born, affect us for our whole lives. And then every moment of our life, we are programmed by our surroundings and experiences.

I would like to give you a thought for you to ponder. The creation of this planet supplies all our needs in a natural form. It is a perfect system when we recognise it. And everywhere is connected to us through our emotions and feelings.

For example, sit by a lake which is still and mirror like, and you feel the calmness. Walk by a stream which is active and you will feel excited and energised. Connect to a tree and really notice everything about it and as you become aware of the strength and power within in, it will give that that feeling of strength and power.

Have you ever looked at the boats and ships in a harbour and wondered where they have been and where they are going to. Pondered how magnificent or neglected they look and how they have been built. Questioned where they could journey and imagined far off places where you could travel in one.

When you go onto a beach by the sea, you feel happiness about the world you live in and the greatness of life. The beach is where you take time away from your normal everyday life.

A building in this world holds memories which are encapsulated in the emotion and feeling of those places. Churches, castles, old buildings all have their own atmosphere created by the people who have lived there before. If you make that feeling connection, you will know whether these are happy or sad buildings, cared for or neglected.

The colours in the building will have an affect on you. Experts in colour therapy know how each colour creates your moods. Bars and pubs would often be coloured red inside. Certain reds are a get up and go colour, so the mood would be one of doing. So drinking and talking and maybe dancing. We know that yellow is a sunshine colour which brightens the mind and gives a feeling of happiness. Green, just like nature, makes us feel good. If you go for a walk in the countryside where green is the predominant colour, you will usually feel healthy after it.

A garden where the flowers are in bloom, where life is abundant, can be a place where you would love to sit and find peace.

The hustle and bustle of a busy village or town would make you feel you should connect with that busy atmosphere. Or a quiet village or town might leave you feeling that not much is happening and leave you at a loss as to what to do.

The benefits of everything in this world are there for us to experience. But we need to notice and not rush by.

Pictures Changing by Themselves

Sometimes as you look at an area "present time", the picture changes in front of you without you making the alterations. When you first arrived at the area "present time" was shown to you but those alterations you see, are the future unfolding and the message here is that you are travelling forward in time. An example might be the "village" changing and your subconscious is showing you the immediate, or soon to be, changes which will happen.

When the Changes You have Instructed Do Not Happen

If when you instruct the subconscious to remove something from the map, it either does not happen or it is difficult for it to be removed, your subconscious is informing you that you need to look more closely at the object or that there is another area of the map which you need to visit because your subconscious is getting mixed messages.

An example might be that a boulder is on top of something which you need to understand and there might be buried something under it. Of course, anything buried anywhere on the map, is because you want to forget about it, so be careful and use ex ray vision first.

Or maybe in a memory in the wood area you were told that life would always be difficult for you and therefore that indoctrination has been unknowingly accepted by you on your subconscious level and your instructions to your subconscious is keeping boulders in the map. This is a mixed message to your subconscious and you need to look at the root cause.

Navigating the Wood

When you go onto the map without a question you are automatically looking in each of the areas, at your life "present time".

When you stand in front of the wood you are looking at yourself right now and the aspects of who you are at the moment are represented by the type of trees and their condition.

When you elevate above the canopy of the trees, the area behind is "the past relevant to present time", and not the whole of your past. So an example would be that you see that the trees have been devastated or destroyed or that there is a clearing which would mean all the trees were not only destroyed or chopped down but completely removed. Remember those trees were you, and whatever they represented in the past in your life, is still affecting you if you are seeing it from just above.

It may be that there is a swamp which would mean you were "swamped". Swamp means to overwhelm or flood with water and, of course, water is always emotion and because the trees will have barely, if at all, survived, that is what happened to you. You were destroyed by the emotion of that situation. Knowing where the water came from gives extra understanding to the situation which you need to understand what to do about it, and asking how old you were at the time, or when this happened, will also help you understand the picture.

Another example may be that you see a jungle and again, in your past, you will have gone through a time in your life where you would have been in a very competitive or complex situation which left you lost in the tangled vegetation where you had a feeling of danger, surrounded by wild animals (people). The law of the jungle would have been the situation you experienced, where those who are strongest and most selfish will be most successful.

A dictionary is a useful tool to understand words like swamp or jungle and will give you the information and understanding you need.

Maybe there is darkness there. A situation where you were in the dark meaning you did not understand the situation and could not see clearly what was happening. Maybe there is an area which you describe as black meaning negative and maybe there is a fear of a monster in there. Asking the subconscious who the monster is, will give you a clear answer.

When you have entered the map you are in a light altered state of consciousness and your thoughts and feelings and experiences will be information for the conscious you from the subconscious. So just asking what something is will give you the answer in the form of thoughts and knowing.

The reason why it is better to look from above is only sensible. If you just walked into the wood, you would not see the whole picture and you may be walking into a jungle or swamp or darkness or meeting up with that monster. You will not be able to see the extent or size of the swamp or jungle. Being so close to the picture achieves nothing except reliving the experience and you need to be a distance and detached from the experience to be able to deal with it on the map. By walking into the wood you would probably also walk into the feeling of not knowing what to do about it because you obviously did not deal with it at the time or it would not be there shown as problems.

Each area of the map is individual and when in the wood area or just elevated above the trees, everything shown there is relevant to it. So fields, meadows, buildings, villages, a lake, mountains etc. are all information of experiences which affected you and who you were in the past, or in the present if at the front of the wood,. It is only when you fly high above the map or view it from the side of the hill that you are able to see all of the areas on the map.

The whole area of you wood should have trees. Wherever there are none it is information where, either you could not be you and develop you, so no trees grew, or, you were destroyed, cut down, or removed.

Obviously if there is a lake in your wood, either the trees which were there could not survive or there was no opportunity to plant trees at that time. Knowing where the water came from which created the lake is a question to ask. Did it come from rain meaning outside emotion which drowned you, in which case remove the rain or storm clouds from the sky as well as the lake, or did it come from underground, in which case you would need to find where it originated to be able to remove the lake. If the rain clouds or underground source is not removed or stopped, then the lake will just reappear. It just requires logic to connect the dots, by which I mean understand the whole story and picture. And then after removing the obstructions, prepare the ground and replant. This will give you your confidence and strength back which you lost or never had.

There is normally no problem if you need to go down into the wood from above the trees to have a closer look but be careful not to get too close to the picture and experience, or it might cause you to feel the experience again. An example might be confusion or fear.

Would there ever be a time when you would walk "into" the wood? Yes! If you go onto the map with a question your subconscious will either, change the whole wood and show you how the picture was in the past relevant to the question or, you will be guided to walk into the wood to a point where your subconscious can take you to a particular memory in the past. Wherever you stop in the wood, there in front of you will be an answer or the answer to your question. Your subconscious has gone through its stored filing system to find what you need to know.

It is also possible to walk into the future in the wood. For example, if you saw a path leading into the wood, this would be showing you that there is an opportunity presented right now, a path to take, which is relevant to you as a person. So it would be possible to follow that path to see where it will go and where you will go in the future if you take that opportunity in your life. Of course it could lead nowhere, but at least you will have that information.

Awareness of other Countries on the Map.

If you become aware of a country in some area of the map, you can use it as a symbol. For example, America may mean "New Frontiers", Japan might represent being steeped in tradition dating back millennia yet thundering ahead. Iceland may represent cold and isolated with the potential of sudden eruptions. Whichever country you see or are aware of, you will find the answer when you research it. Canada is a variation of culture and etiquette split into two.

Know Who You Are

The discovery of this amazing world within you connects you to all that you are and can be. You are the Life and the Power of the Universe. There are no restrictions once you open to Truth.

What is Truth

Truth will be to each person what they can accept. To truly know Truth, all previous beliefs may need to be removal. Are you willing to let them go if they are not "Truth"?

The Subconscious Will Answer You.

While you are journeying on the map, when you see a symbol you do not understand, you can mentally ask your subconscious what it is or what it means. The first thought which comes to your mind will be the answer. Your Subconscious is quite capable of speaking to you telepathically.

It is for you to build your relationship with this part of you, and you do that by talking to it either through the symbol of an expert or talking to the pictures you see. Talk to a tree, a rock, water, the path, the building, the boats and the answer to your question will come into your mind. At first this seems a strange thing to do but when you are on the map, you are in an altered state of consciousness and that consciousness is completely connected to you and you are one. Nothing is there which is not information, but unless you ask what everything represents, the answer is limited. Enjoy meeting this part of yourself. It really is you and it will help you reach your goal through symbolic consciousness mentoring..

Scientific Experiments

I recently read an article where three different studies were done by different teams of scientists on DNA samples. They discovered something which defies the conventional laws of physics.

They came to a stunning realisation that our emotions affect our DNA and our DNA literally shape the behaviour of the light photons that make up the world around us and therefore shapes the world around us.

So DNA = Subconscious store of information = the mind map = affect on the world around us and our life.

ABOUT THE AUTHOR

MY JOURNEY TO DISCOVER THE MAP TO THE UNIVERSE WITHIN

I was born in a terraced house in Middlesbrough in the North East of England in 1948 and I lived in that same house until I married at the age of 21. My father was a painter and decorator and my mother was a school cook. My father's family lived in the next street and, unbeknown to me throughout my early years, were brought up as Spiritualists. At that time people did not speak openly about Mediumship and Spiritualism because of an archaic law (the Witchcraft Act of 1735) which meant meetings were considered illegal and therefore had to be held in secret. During the Second World War, this act was used to imprison a number of mediums and this Act was still in place right up to 1951 when it was replaced by the Fraudulent Mediums Act. My mother later explained to me that she did not like what she called "mixing with the dead" and so any talk about it was banned in our house.

However, even as a young child I had an awareness of discarnate people being in my home, but if I mentioned it my mother she would tell me I was imagining it and so I grew up with these visions and sometimes physical apparitions believing that they were not real and only my imagination.

On my insistence, from the age of eight, I attended a Church of England Sunday school and services and even joined the choir and my mother was not pleased about that because it interfered with family Sunday outings. Being a good orthodox Christian at that time, I started to get up very early to attend the 7am Service so that our family day was not interfered with. Like many, I had a dream of being a nun and going to Africa to heal and save the people from whatever ills they had in their life and this dream stayed with me until I was 15 years old. At 15 I felt as if I did not fit in the world and felt so separate that I decided to step into the world "reality" like everyone else and shut down the "imaginary" visions and experiences.

I left school at the age of 15 and worked in a Wallpaper and Paint shop and attended Art College in the evenings for interior and textile design. This was the 1960s and my tutor at the college suggested that there were very few opportunities for work available for the many that were in the new age/hippie era who were into art and so he thought I should train to be a college art lecturer. My school years had been at a secondary school and the education was aimed at working class employment. Women were still expected to get married, have children and be housewives so stretching their academic capabilities was not on the curriculum. The point was that I did not have the education from school to achieve becoming a teacher without many years filling the education gaps missed, so I let that idea go, left my shop job and instead attended a secretarial college where I learned short hand and typing and comptometer operating.

I had married at the age of 21, which was an age any young lady was expected to be married in the North East of England. Generally it was thought that if you were not married by then, you were on the shelf and no man would want you. Many of my friends were married at 18 years old. I had talked to my husband about my parents looking to buy a hotel in Blackpool, Lancashire, when I was younger and that I was disappointed that they never actually did it and I wondered if he and I could do that one day. Eventually he thought it would be a good idea and we started our search for a hotel to buy, first in the Lake District and then in the South West of England. I left my job at the shipping company.

After two years in the first hotel in Torquay, we sold up and bought a sea front hotel in Paignton which was the next town along the coast. There were 24 letting bedrooms, a functions room and outdoor swimming pool and we accommodated mainly elderly coach holiday groups except for the July and August school holidays when we took bookings from what we called "privates" or individual couples and families.

I had for as long as I remember had a very strong feeling that I would die when I was 32 years old and even told close friends. It did not bother me but as I approached that age, one particular friend told me that she was worried that I would die because I seemed so sure. I now had my 32nd birthday but instead of dying, it was as if the old me was gone and I stepped into a new era.

To explain the beginning of that happening, I was in the hotel reception and received a phone call from a gentleman who with his wife was travelling from the east coast of England and their car had broken down in the midlands so he was letting me know that they would arrive a day later than they had booked. It was strange but I was disappointed that his wife, who I had not spoken to, would not be arriving that day as expected. The next day when they did arrive I felt that his wife, Pauline, was like a long lost friend even though I had not met her before and I had to hold back from wrapping my arms around her to welcome her. Pauline, likewise told me later that she had felt the same.

Then it all started. That evening when I went to bed it was as if my awareness of the spirit world and my visions which I had closed down when I was 15, came back with a vengeance. I could hear loud voices and see and feel the presence of people from the spirit world. For a moment I thought I was going mad. I even left my body and was invited by a spirit communicator to travel down a dark tunnel, at the end of which was a bright light. I remembered wondering how it was possible to travel so fast along the tunnel and then when I saw the light I said to myself, "I have heard of tunnels with lights at the end of them, being seen by people when they die". I catapulted back into my body, left my body again and was hovering over it and then decided I had better try to get back into it. I managed it and can only describe the feeling as trying to bury myself in soft soil. Not the most comfortable experience.

The next day I found myself relaying what had happened to me to Pauline, and she seemed unfazed by my story. She told me that she was a Spiritual Healer and she suggested that we both went to visit Paignton Spiritualist Church which was only a short walk away from the hotel. I felt as if she was my safety net, helping me discover again that I was a medium. It was as if our meeting was all planned. Throughout those early days we seemed to have a telepathic link and after she returning home she would often phone me to see how I was doing.

Over the next few years I met up with Pauline at the Arthur Findlay Residential College at Stansted Hall, a manor house which had been left to the Spiritualist National Union by Arthur Findlay for the use of training Psychics and Mediums.

After the mediumship demonstration at the Church we went to a nearby pub for a drink and there were a lot of Spiritualists there who had been to the meeting and they welcomed us. That was the beginning of my relationship with the Spiritualist church.

I started to attend the Open Circle at the church on a Wednesday night, which was run by a brilliant medium and Spiritualist Minister called Lillian Hurst. People were allowed to come in and sit in a circle for an hour and use it as a practice ground. Each week Lillian said "I will open the circle in prayer, then you can meditate for 15 minutes and then I will open the circle and you can each individually work". Being new to this, I wondered what she meant by meditate so after a few weeks I asked her what I was supposed to be doing as a meditation. Looking back, I know she linked with the spirit world as she told me "imagine being in a garden and from there walk past a wood to a lake and then come back".

This I did each week but then noticed that the pictures I was imagining were changing and this was the beginning of my discovering what I first called a Self Discovery Meditation and which would eventually be called "The Linda Bullock Technique™" and "The Mind Map of the Subconscious".

I was so excited to discover during the time I spent at the church that everything I had been aware of through my childhood and youth was real and that it was my ability to connect with the Spirit World.

My development as a medium began at that church and after a while I was invited into a "Closed Development Circle" to train and develop my gift to become a working medium. I was still coming to terms with the understanding that what we were doing was called "Mental Mediumship" and that I would not necessarily see the spirit world as solid, which I had when I was younger. I liken the process of development to learning to play the piano. I learned that I had a vocation to do the work no matter what obstacles I encountered and I eventually started to take bookings as an inspirational speaker and demonstrator for divine services and public demonstrations in other churches and centres in the south west of England and eventually further afield in other countries.

My interest in the subject also encouraged me to develop as a spiritual, hands on healer and trance medium. Trance mediumship is allowing a spirit guide to speak through the medium. I eventually became a healer, and healing trainer and assessor with Healer Practitioners Association International. (HPAI).

Each year for a week and weekend for 15 years I attended the Arthur Findlay College and learned so much from some of the greatest mediums including Gordon Higginson, Glyn Edwards, Albert Best, Mavis Pattilla, Eric Hatton and so many others who I hold in high regard. They were my tutors and inspirers, who laid the foundation of my ability to work with the Spirit World and share the wonderful truth that there is no death, that life in eternal and that our loved ones are never far away and are still interested in us and our lives.

In 1999 at the age of 49 I became a tutor at that amazing college and was able to share my knowledge with those who came to discover their capabilities.

Earlier at Paignton Spiritualist Church I had been voted by the membership to become the President and the following year I set up a teaching system within the church, sharing all I had discovered over the years. I ran most of the circles and groups myself at first but, as the spirit world told me, "from the students there would come the teachers" and this is exactly what happened. Within the teaching system I set up was still the Open Circle, but added to that was a Healers Open Circle, an awareness group with over 40 Students attending each year and travelled up to a hundred miles each week to attend, an Intermediate Group, eventually Three Development Circles, a Beginners Trance Circle, a Meditation Group, an Inspiration and Philosophy Circle and when students showed signs of being inspired to use art with their mediumship, there was a Spirit Art Group. These circles were the foundation for helping many mediums to develop their gifts and for teachers to set up their own circles in their own churches and centres in the South West of England.

All the time the Linda Bullock Technique™ (LBT) was expanding and developing but at first I had only used it as an analysis tool. It wasn't until 1999 that I discovered I could also use it to reprogram my life and help others with it but it took a while for me to realise how amazing it was.

From those first three areas I had started with which were inspired by Lillian Hurst, other areas showed themselves. I was learning the language of the subconscious, discovering that the mind map took me to communicate with that aspect of myself. There was the wood representing my strengths and weaknesses and who I had become from my experiences, the stream area representing my emotions and the lake area representing balance and harmony within me and showing me my health and wisdom gained through my life experiences. But also I was learning that there were time lines which I could navigate to. Within those areas and time lines were not only present time states but also the past and the future. And then I had discovered areas which represented my material world including my home life and working and social life. I could see how every moment of my life was recorded within my subconscious in its own language and I was learning that language. I realised that every experience I had ever had became the programming of my life, and that programming was creating my own reality without my previously realising it.

And then there appeared areas which connected me to the spirit world, my family and friends who had passed on, my spiritual advisor. There was also a connection to the earth and the universe where all questions I had could be answered. And then I discovered my own spirit and the group soul I was connected with and came from and I learned how to communicate with them. And then there was the connection to the God consciousness and beyond. The words "all the answers are within" now made perfect sense as the mind map showed me the way to the answers to any questions I had about my life, the world and unlimited knowledge.

I had taken a weekend booking as a medium at Stourbridge Spiritualist Church and apart from taking the Divine Service, demonstrating mediumship at two public meetings and giving private sittings, they invited me to run a workshop seminar on the LBT. One of the people who attended was a counsellor/therapist called Graham and he realised that he could use the technique to help some of his clients. We agreed to communicate with each other and with the client's permission discuss what they had seen on their mind map and the changes they could make and the results of those changes were often immediate. Graham persuaded me that it was important for me to share my discovery because, as he put it, "it will help many people". I decided I should ask the spirit world for their advice as I did not have the time and energy to do everything. With that question in mind, I travelled to the group soul light and heard them say "you came to bring this technique to the earth". So the decision was made.

I put my mediumship work on hold and began to discover how far I could take the technique. I practiced on friends and anyone who was willing to experiment with it with me. I particularly loved working with my granddaughter when she was six years old. My daughter had said that she seemed to be worried but was unable to share what was troubling her with her mother so I offered to put her to bed and decided because of her young age that I would let her create her mind map. A few years later I discovered that her areas on the map replicated exactly the LBT map. I asked her to close her eyes and I would tell her a story which I began "Once upon a time in a far away land there was a magic kingdom and the ruler of that magic kingdom was Princess Lauren"

One of the areas she wanted to visit was to a light house, so I thought I would ask her if there was a harbour nearby and if there were any boats in it. She answered that there was a harbour with boats in it but all the boats had holes in them. I asked her what had caused the holes in the boats and she said that the fish had bitten them. So here was the story of what was happening to her. The boats represented her school work and the fish were "hidden knowledge" meaning knowledge which she had to learn but was struggling with. Thus just as the boats showed, she was sinking and struggling to keep afloat and cope with the work.

I suggested that she instruct that she is the ruler and that the fish are not allowed to bite the boats, then I said she must instruct workmen to fix the boats so they were sea worthy. She said she could see them doing the work and she decided what colours to have each of them painted. And then, without her even knowing what the pictures represented, she said she asked for gold stars to be put all over them. The next day, she came home from school with a certificate, and yes, on the certificate was a gold star. About six months later, because my son in law was unable to get time off work, I went with my daughter to meet Lauren's teacher and as we entered the room she said "Oh yes, Lauren. In all the years I have been a teacher I have never seen this before. In the last six months Lauren has gone from level 4 and had achieved the much higher grade of level 21". I know that the changes made to her subconscious mind map had helped her achieve that.

My former colleague and tutor at the Arthur Findlay College, Sheila French, was running residential seminars in a hotel in Folkestone in Kent and kindly invited me to join them and offer private LBT sittings to her students, helping them to build their confidence and overcome obstacles which were preventing them from becoming their full potential. From there I received a number of invitations to centres in Germany, Switzerland and Austria to train Practitioners to use the technique for their clients.

By now I had created a whole training system for Practitioners who were using the technique in their clinics, offering one to one therapy sessions. The website created for the technique lists those who are recognised Practitioners and some of the Practitioners are becoming LBT trainers.

For more information about the technique, Linda, other LBT practitioners and events/seminar dates, please visit: **www.lindabullocktechnique.com**